MONARCH FILM STUDIES

King Vidor

John Baxter

MONARCH PRESS

Standard Book Number: 671-08103-9

Library of Congress Catalog Card Number: 75-23544

Designed by Denise Biller

Published by
MONARCH PRESS
a division of Simon & Schuster, Inc.
1 West 39th Street
New York, N.Y. 10018

CONTENTS

AUTHOR

JOHN BAXTER is the author of numerous books on film, including *The Cinema of John Ford, An Appalling Talent: Ken Russell,* and *Stunt: The Story of the Great Movie Stunt Men.* He contributes regularly to the *London Times* and *Sunday Times Magazine.*

ACKNOWLEDGMENTS

I particularly want to thank the libraries and individuals who made it possible for me to see many of King Vidor's films not in general circulation, notably William K. Everson, Eileen Bowser and Charles Silver of the Museum of Modern Art in New York, Jeremy Boulton of the National Film Archive of the British Film Institute, and John Kuiper and Pat Sheehan of the Library of Congress, Washington, D.C. Special thanks must go to Kathleen Cheesmond and to Vidor for his generosity in answering the questions of yet another devotee.

In researching this book, I was assisted by material contained in the special King Vidor issue of *Positif* magazine (September 1974) and by Bernard Cohn's perceptive interview with the director.

Quotations have also been taken from: *Popcorn Venus* by Marjorie Rosen (Coward, McCann and Geoghegan, New York, 1973), and *Laurette* by Marguerite Courtney (Rinehart and Company, New York, 1955), as well as Vidor's two books, *A Tree Is a Tree* (Harcourt Brace, New York, 1952) and *On Film Making* (W. H. Allen, London, 1973).

Photographs are courtesy of the following: Barrie Pattison, *The Film Journal*, the Memory Shop, Cinemabilia, the Film Stills Archive of the Museum of Modern Art, and the Stills Archive of the British Film Institute.

Hard riding and soft religion don't mix, so get goin'.
—Title in Vidor's *The Sky Pilot*.

King Vidor in 1931 on the set of ***Street Scene***

PREFACE

For the last decade King Vidor, a lover of Europe, has been conveniently at large, turning up unannounced at the Venice Film Festival, attending a retrospective of his work at San Sebastian, spending a few days in London promoting a recent book — courtly, a little aloof, often accompanied by his friend Colleen Moore but more often alone, a quiet and slightly stooped man of nearly eighty whose Texas good manners are undented by even the most formal interviewers. Yet the published material on this acknowledged master of the American cinema is sparse. Too diverse, too operatic, perhaps too American for the average European critic who can know only by hearsay of the impact of his last silent films like *The Big Parade* and *The Crowd,* he daunts the new writer and often bores experts who think that, in acknowledging *The Big Parade* as an anti-war classic and *Duel in the Sun* as a sex-and-Selznick spectacular, they have summed up his talent. But his sixty features cover a broad range of the cinema; and Vidor, with his dogged control over his work, has made each one the powerful statement of an acute intelligence. His development from the rural school of Griffith through the new American realism to the revealing personal statement of *Ruby Gentry* concentrates in one career the growth of the American cinema.

Based on conversations recorded in London late in 1974, and on interviews not previously published in English, this book is offered with respect to a man who, by any reasonable criterion, is among the greatest filmmakers of modern times.

A DEMONIC LANDSCAPE

There is a sense in which all American film is geographic. No national cinema places more emphasis on the outdoors, or more intimately relates the attitudes and preoccupations of its characters to the shape and symbology of the land. Almost every major work of American silent cinema has its component of landscape, and classics abound in which nature assumes a power and mystical significance: *Way Down East, Greed, The Wind, The Iron Horse, The Salvation Hunters, The Gold Rush, The General* and *Sunrise* are obvious examples.

By adopting the traditions of Europe and the stage in the late twenties, Hollywood largely extinguished this sense, but for some directors it remained a lifelong preoccupation. John Ford in particular filled his films with a sense of landscape as metaphor, so that one can read his message in the precise manipulation of landscape forms. Rivers correspond to peace, dust to dissolution, storms to internal conflict, the pinnacles of Monument Valley to the precepts by which his cavalrymen, guardians of moral order, lead their lives of quiet duty.

It is to this family of filmmakers — the clan of Griffith, Walsh and Ford — that King Vidor belongs. In a long and active career he has preserved his personal style from commercial erosion and retained well into the sixties the sense of American landscape which distinguishes his best films. What sets Vidor apart from his contemporaries in this gentle field is, however, a dark, almost demonic view of the land. Where Ford, even at his most engaged, remains relaxed and affectionate towards his subjects, Vidor sees America in another light, that of a treacherous and actively hostile environment in which one survives only by struggle and sacrifice.

If Ford's characteristic landscape is the desert, Vidor's is the swamp. While Ford interests himself in the resolution of conflict in terms of moral choices and acquiescence to destiny and duty, Vidor deals in obsession and conflicts often resolved in terms of mutual destruction. He represents better than any other filmmaker the current of violence in American art which wells up in social protest, often in the wake of some cultural upheaval.

Hallelujah

Northwest Passage

The Big Parade, his most famous early work, is less a film about war than an attack — admittedly romanticized — on jingoism and the public indifference to returning veterans. *Japanese War Bride* is equally disenchanted about the ability of America to accept the cessation of the Korean War. *The Crowd* and *Street Scene* reflect the cynicism of Dos Passos, Lawson and other leftist authors at a time when optimism was the prevailing capitalist view. *Duel in the Sun* and *Man Without a Star* mock romantic views of the West, showing frontier life as the scene of bigotry, violence, and greed.

Running through all Vidor's work is a sense of the earth itself as a snare and a delusion, ready to suck down those who walk on its surface. The plethora of swamp scenes in Vidor's films can hardly be a coincidence — they occupy an important role in *Wild Oranges, The Big Parade, Hallelujah, Northwest Passage* and *Ruby Gentry* — while dramatic scenes by rivers or lakes appear in scores of his other films, always with the emphasis on water as a destroyer. In *The Jack Knife Man* a river carries away the old man's houseboat; the central fight between David Butler and John Bowers in *The Sky Pilot* takes place by a river; *Bird of Paradise*, with its South Seas setting, makes significant use of the ocean's moods; *Northwest Passage* is set almost entirely outdoors, with the river on one occasion almost destroying Rogers Rangers' expedition to subdue savage Indians. *Duel in the Sun* celebrates every aspect of the American western landscape from pools and rivers to the dust and rocks of Indian Head rock, where a hideous face rears up out of the desert to oversee Pearl's homicidal reunion with Lewt. The murders and adultery of *Beyond the Forest* have a rural setting, *Japanese War Bride* a California coastal location, while in *Ruby Gentry* characters and landscape are intimately related.

Asked about this element of *Ruby Gentry*, Vidor remarked, "There's one scene I like a lot in the film, because it corresponds to something vital. It's the scene where the girl has the barrage demolished. At the moment when the earth is flooded, the man is destroyed. All his ambitions crumble. I think there was a fine symbol there. . . . The conflict between the man who is trying to build himself up and to build something, and this brutal destruction, seemed good to us. In the film, by the way, water kills twice. First it kills Jim Gentry, who drowns, then it kills the hope of Boake Tackman. It's the reverse of *Our Daily Bread*, where the water was a savior."

King Wallis Vidor was born in Galveston, Texas, in 1894, the son of Charles Vidor, then a dealer in South American lumber. "King," Vidor confirmed, "is my real name. I had an uncle by the name of King. He was my mother's favorite brother. The Vidor is Hungarian. My grandfather emigrated to Texas in 1865. He was a press agent for a famous Hungarian violinist named Rimini." Vidor's childhood recollections vacillate between those of Peacock Military Academy in San Antonio, which he "hated," and more pleasant times taking and developing portraits of relatives on a box Brownie earned with singing in the church choir and selling *The Saturday Evening Post* door to door. He dates his first instinct towards movie-making from a moment when, at the age of ten, he sensed the "rhythm, tempo, beauty, humor" in the movement of other boys diving from a platform into Galveston Bay — a moment, significantly, dominated by water.

Equally revelatory was an early exposure to Christian Science, of which he was a lifelong adherent. "As a small child I had been very ill. I had been affected by a nervous illness. I saw many doctors whose diagnoses were very uncertain. It was from then on that I took an interest in Christian Science. My mother was interested in Christian Science. Thanks to what she told me about (it) I was able to establish what were the real links between what happened within me and the outside world." The blend of pragmatic self-help and religious mysticism implicit in Mary Baker Eddy's teaching often appeared in Vidor's films.

As a teenager Vidor became ticket-taker and projectionist at a Galveston cinema, from which he graduated to making amateur newsreels and finally his first two-reeler, *In Tow*, a comedy set against the background of car races held on a beach near his home town. He also worked on two one-reel comedies made by Edward Sedgwick, then a minor comic but later to be a considerable Hollywood director. *In Tow* and a documentary which followed on the sugar industry featured a local actress named Florence Arto, later Vidor's wife. It was with Florence and Sedgwick that Vidor set off from Galveston in 1915 to drive to California in a Model T Ford, hoping for employment in Hollywood and expecting to finance the trip by shooting footage for the Ford Company's advertising newsreel.

The profits from Ford proved illusory and the journey was both uncomfortable and expensive, but during it Vidor became confirmed in his vision of America. In almost every interview throughout the next sixty years he was to extol the pleasure of travelling with a small unit in one or two cars, stopping whenever a scene or a setting struck him. Later, he spoke nostalgically of "my early days in Hollywood, when the whole company had gone on location in one seven passenger Packard automobile. At the time I was the assistant director and was expected to act as chauffeur as well. The director occupied the other front seat; then came the cameraman and his assistant on the two folding jump seats, and in the rear seat the cast — two stars and a character man. The Bell and Howell camera was strapped to the running board on one side and the camera tripod on the other. If the director saw a maple tree alive with the golden hues of a late afternoon sun, he would stop, and while the cameraman and his assistant set up the equipment, *ad lib* a love scene that would later allow any theatre organist to give vent to the full power of his romantic imagination." He would sometimes spot a useful location from a train, "a part of the landscape that called out to me," and return to use it in a film. His love of natural light and locations is essentially that of a documentarist and, both through his friendship with Robert Flaherty and Pare Lorentz and his own early background as a newsreel cameraman, all Vidor's films were to have a quality of documentary realism wedded always to his sense of nature's latent violence.

A MESSAGE TO HUMANITY:
THE EARLY SILENT FEATURES

Vidor had no immediate opportunity to put his documentary skill nor, for that matter, his other artistic abilities into action when they reached Hollywood. Broke and stranded in San Francisco, he and Florence lived off breakfast cereal scraps found in grocer's boxes and free condensed milk samples handed out at the Panama-Pacific International Exposition. (The Italian plaster workers imported to build the Fair's pavilions were even then working for Griffith in Hollywood on the towering sets for *Intolerance*.) Years before, Vidor had given a letter of introduction to a young Texas actress named Corinne Griffith who, with the help of Vidor's Californian cousin, had landed an extra job with Vitagraph. Now an established star, Miss Griffith got Florence a screen test; shot by Charles Rosher, Mary Pickford's brilliant cameraman, it earned her an immediate contract with Thomas Ince, and she went on to become a familiar face in Vitagraph comedies. The less-attractive King had to be content with occasional scenario sales and a minor office job with Universal, lost when the company discovered that the scripts sold to them by "Charles K. Wallis" were in fact by one of its clerks.

Fred Turner in ***The Jack Knife Man***

Now out of a job, and conveniently exempt from the rule that employees could not hold two posts at once, he became a regular free-lance scenarist for Universal and also directed a series of independent shorts featuring Judge William Brown, a Salt Lake City magistrate whose unusual methods of rehabilitating juvenile offenders had earned some notoriety. But Vidor failed in his attempt to gain a foothold on feature filmmaking by splicing together a number of these two-reelers.

It was not until 1918 that he found a backer for his first feature; a group of doctors and dentists affiliated as the Brentwood Film Corporation financed Vidor's own scenario of, paradoxically, a Christian Science tract called *The Turn in the Road.* "The production is frankly a preachment," noted the *New York Times,* but singled out as particularly powerful a scene significant in the light of Vidor's disquiet about natural forces. It contrasts the reaction to a thunderstorm of a child and a rich, powerful man. "The child is shown, half-sitting, looking out the window at the storm. He is interested and apparently it does not occur to him to be afraid. Each flash of lightning illuminates his radiant innocent face. The man is shown sitting in his luxurious library. At each flash of lightning and instinctively imagined crash of thunder he winces, shies as it were, in fear of forces which his money and power cannot overcome."

Vidor made three more films for the Brentwood Corporation, the first a romantic comedy called *Better Times* (1919) featuring the then-unknown comedienne Zasu Pitts, whom the director spotted on a Hollywood streetcar, and the equally obscure David Butler who, as actor and director, had a long movie career. Miss Pitts played "an unloved wallflower in a boarding school writing to and supposedly receiving letters from a big league ball player. Just when her grand deception is about to be discovered, a famous ball player actually falls in love with her." The last two films, *The Other Half* (1919) and *Poor Relations* (1919), also featuring Miss Pitts, starred Florence Vidor, by then a rising star. In 1920, Vidor regarded his duty done by Brentwood and signed with First National, a new exhibitors' group trying to break the major studio stranglehold on product, to make two features. $15,000 of Vidor's $75,000 advance from First National went to build his own studio, "Vidor Village," on Santa Monica Boulevard; he marked the event in the January 1920 issue of *Variety* with a ringing "Creed and Pledge":

1. *I believe in the motion picture that carries a message to humanity.*

2. *I believe in the picture that will help humanity to free itself from the shackles of fear and suffering that have so long bound it with iron chains.*
3. *I will not knowingly produce a picture that contains anything I do not believe to be absolutely true to human nature, anything that could injure anyone or anything unclean in thought or action.*
4. *Nor will I deliberately portray anything to cause fright, suggest fear, glorify mischief, condone cruelty or extenuate malice.*
5. *I will never picture evil or wrong, except to prove the fallacy of its line.*
6. *So long as I direct pictures, I will make only those founded upon principles of right, and I will endeavor to draw upon the inexhaustible source of good for my stories, my guidance and my inspiration.*

First National might have guessed from this manifesto that Vidor would not supply the gay comedies starring Mrs. Vidor which they expected, and predictably *The Jack Knife Man* (1920), though based on a story by Ellis Parker Butler, author of the comedy success *Pigs Is Pigs*, had little humor. Instead Vidor offered a bleak story of river life in which, though his wife has a small part, the lead is taken by aged stage actor Fred Turner. Peter Lane (Turner) lives alone on a rickety shanty-boat until a woman staggers into his home at the height of a storm and, dying almost immediately, leaves him in charge of her little boy. Moved by love for the child and helped by a kindly socialite (Florence Vidor), he turns his hobby of carving toy animals into a profession and marries the widow who had her cap set for him all along.

Vidor undercuts the humor and sentiment with a bitter sense of the wintry Mississippi landscape (recreated at Stockton, California) and the hard rural life. Leafless trees and ragged saplings line the grey river on which Lane moors his boat, and the river threatens to tear it from its moorings. A spectacular scene had been planned in which the boat is caught in the disintegrating ice, but when Vidor returned to shoot it the thaw had already begun;

shortly after, Griffith released *Way Down East* with its famous chase on the frozen river. The sudden appearance of the woman and child at the height of a thunderstorm, with flares of lightning and an alarm clock shrilling to terrify the boy, recalls Vidor's ambivalence towards nature. Occasionally Butler's rural humor shows through, particularly in the scenes with the tramp Booge (Harry Todd) who competes with Lane for the boy's affection. "Why did he take the alarm clock?" the boy asks when Lane leaves quietly to pawn his only valuable possession.

"I guess he thought I'd steal it."

"Would you have stole it?"

"I guess so."

But the general tone of relentless realism, unredeemed by Lane's eventual prosperity and marriage, chilled First National even more than Vidor's returning the unused $11,000 of the budget. "The First National Exhibitors didn't want me to save money, but to spend it. They had huge theatres to fill and they wanted names, big names, and more names."

This experience had a fundamental effect on Vidor's attitude to filmmaking. Thereafter the "preachment" complained of in *The Turn in the Road* and the ideals of his "Creed and Pledge" receded. His next film for First National, *The Family Honor* (1920), starred Florence and apparently stuck closer to the traditional comedy/romance style of the time. For the five years during which he struggled, finally without success, to keep Vidor Village alive in a community increasingly dominated by the big combines, his films, though distinguished, were almost entirely the romances and comedies then in vogue. Hoping to avoid total commitment to stage-bound material, he made *The Sky Pilot* (1921) a spectacular, combining dramatic scenery with a cattle stampede and a comic Western story in the hope of pleasing everyone. The sentimental story of a reforming parson in the Canadian backwoods featured John Bowers as Arthur Moore the "sky pilot," and stage star Colleen Moore as the girl he loves and rescues from the careering cattle.

Shot on location in the Truckee River country, *The Sky Pilot* suffered from Vidor's insistence on authentic locations, even when

John Bowers in **The Sky Pilot**

this involved removing the signs of an early snow fall for a "summer" scene, then covering the ground in salt when real snow refused to fall. "Canada! A Land Where Nature Must Glory In Her Handiwork" reads the opening title, but the mountainscapes and snow scenes did not disguise the film's confusion about its market. The romance and comedy work best. As the cowboy Hendricks, who begins as Moore's enemy but becomes his friend, David Butler plays for farce, falling flat on his back at the news of a "sky pilot's" arrival in his wild home town, breaking up the first service by leading in some friends with hands piously joined and finally resolving the tension in a fist fight which ends with Moore, the winner, mopping his adversary's wounds. Hendricks' conversion is believable and touching. "When a man's religion will let him do what you done and live," he says, "there must be something in it." But in general *The Sky Pilot* hovers uneasily between Western comedy and the celebration of landscape which is closest to Vidor's heart.

The high cost of location shooting made *The Sky Pilot* too expensive for a big profit. Though First National released the film, they would not finance any further Vidor productions. Since the spectacular cattle stampede had drawn a lot of attention, he planned and shot an elaborate model scene of a train tumbling into a flooded river from a collapsing trestle, persuading Thomas Ince that a film with such a climax could not help succeeding. Ince agreed to back the film, but typically Vidor used the disaster early in *Love Never Dies* (1921), putting more emphasis on the rural love story (influenced, he agrees, by Griffith) which makes up most of the film.

After his idyllic marriage has been broken up by his wife's father (a theme to recur in *The Crowd*), young architect John Trott leaves the small town of Ridgeville with only an orphan girl and her dog for company. Hoping to start a new life, he reports himself dead in the train crash he survives, and settles down in another town. Years later, he returns to find his wife remarried to a wastrel, whom he nevertheless tries to rescue from the river after a suicide attempt. (The motivation for the suicide is eccentric; after drawing his gun on Trott, the second husband feels his wife could no longer love him after such an act and throws himself into the river in remorse.) The husband dies, and John and Tilly are reunited. Except for a pleasant scene of a barbecue in the Ridgeville town square to celebrate the laying of a foundation stone, and the appearance of the lovely Madge Bellamy as the young wife, *Love Never Dies* is a routine work, though the dramatic use of rivers throughout the film marked a motif that was to become typical of Vidor's work.

Perhaps reluctantly, Vidor settled down to producing and directing films starring Florence; comedies of manners and romantic melodramas of the type Cecil B. DeMille was making popular. (Later he remarked of DeMille, for whom Florence became a regular star later in her career, that his films "make me want to give up directing.") *Conquering the Woman* (1922), an obvious spin-off from DeMille's *Male and Female*, had Florence as a spoiled society girl engaged to a foppish French count, marooned by her irate father on a desert island, from which she is rescued by the cowboy (David Butler) who loves her.

Woman, Wake Up and *The Real Adventure* (both 1922) have earned a place in the history of feminist cinema with their picture of a woman struggling to succeed in a male society. In the first, Florence becomes involved in society to please her husband and is so successful at it that he becomes jealous, while in *The Real Adventure* she is transformed after her marriage to a wealthy husband; she studies law, goes on stage as a chorus girl, designs costumes, opens a salon but realizes that home and family must come first.

In *Dusk to Dawn* (1922), returning to the DeMille format, Vidor used Florence in a double role of a modern city girl and an Indian beggar, interweaving the stories of the latter's life and the former's attempt to save her brother from a forgery charge. Vidor also produced Rowland V. Lee's 1922 version of Booth Tarkington's small town portrait *Alice Adams* in which Florence starred. But *Dusk to Dawn* marked the end of many things for the Vidors. Florence's career, Vidor wrote, "had gone forward so steadily that she was beginning to be known as 'the first lady of the screen' . . . Somewhere along the roads of our divergent professional interests could be found the cause of our estranged personal relationship and subsequent divorce." Shortly after their divorce in 1926, Florence married the violinist Jascha Heifetz.

In 1922, Vidor Village closed down, and Vidor returned to freelancing. Louis B. Mayer's thriving Metro company offered him a touchy task. Since 1912, stage star Laurette Taylor had been playing the impish Irish teenager Peg O'Connell in *Peg o' My Heart,* written by her husband J. Hartley Manners, and Mayer had now persuaded the thirty-eight-year-old actress to reproduce the role for movies. He chose Vidor to direct.

According to Miss Taylor's biographer, Marguerite Courtney, in *Laurette,* "It was a very gloomy young man who waited at the station to greet the famous Broadway actress upon her arrival in Hollywood. He had seen the tests sent out from the East. They had

Laurette Taylor in **Peg O' My Heart**

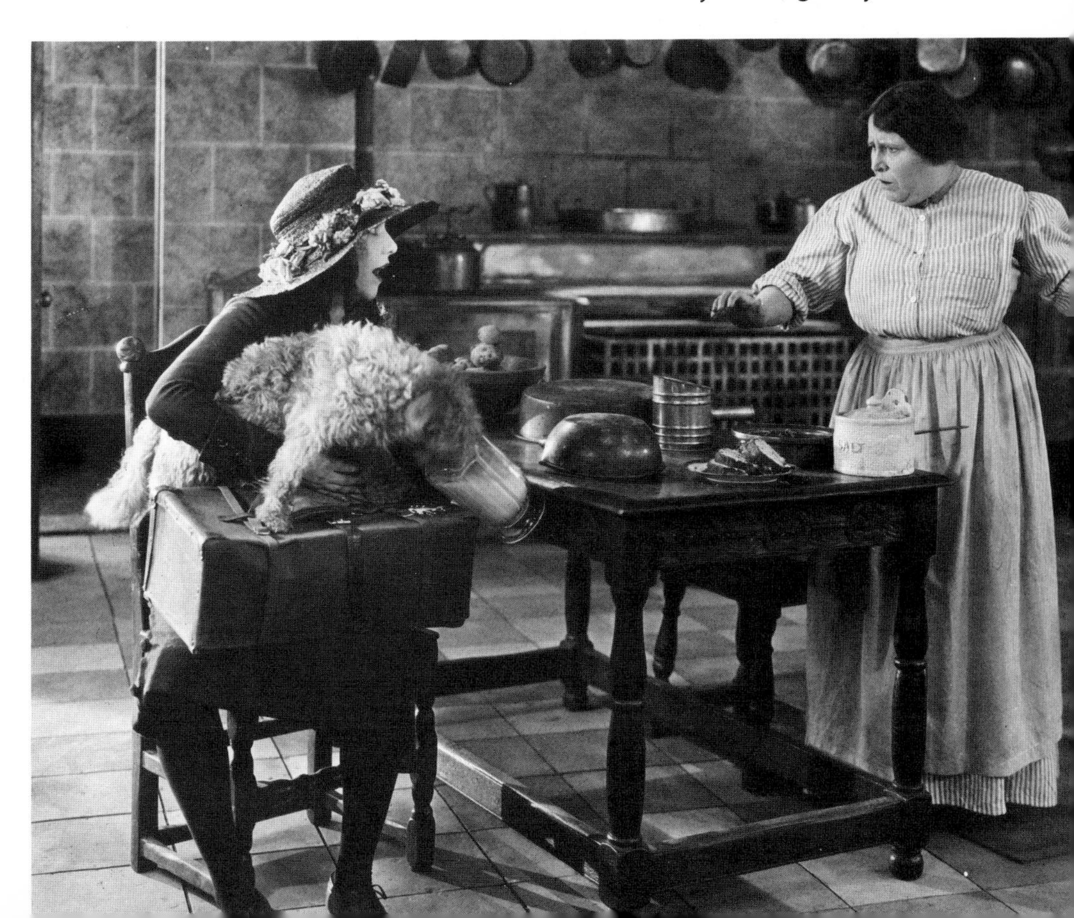

been made under the supervision of David Wark Griffith and with that illustrious name attached to them, Vidor had no cause to think that they were other than the best possible. But in frowsy wig and dead white makeup the famous star looked closer to forty than eighteen. At the first sight of Laurette he experienced acute relief. She came toward him smiling, and his camera-minded eye saw at once a face all round and animated, essentially youthful. Pumping her hand he burst out impulsively, 'For heaven's sake, let's make a test with your own lovely hair.' "

Too diplomatic to explain that the blinding light and limited resolution of film stocks at the time made it impossible adequately to cut twenty years from a woman's age, Vidor ignored the tests shot by Billy Bitzer and used a modified stills lens and carefully focused lighting to disguise Miss Taylor's age. She looks, if not teenaged, then at least youthful enough to pass as the Irish orphan boarded out on a group of stuffy English aristocrats, whose lives she and her dog Othello illuminate by her casual good humor.

Manners, disliking the script, rewrote it entirely to restore much of the stuffy stage quality, and also "supervised" the production. Vidor, however, had all the problems. He could eradicate some signs of age but not the habits of a lifetime which made her performance a riot of scene-stealing mannerisms. Friends of the star dropped in periodically to suggest new scenes; one in which Peg looks for a flea on her dog was created by Douglas Fairbanks. Her movements are exaggerated, her performance spotted with bits of business — blowing her nose becomes a production, with the handkerchief being folded and re-folded, tucked under her belt, and fastened with a safety pin; she even picks something from her teeth before proceeding with the next scene. Except for a striking shot of her father's Irish cottage and some exteriors in a formal garden (both shot in the San Fernando Valley), the film confines itself to a mansion set identical with that for the play on Broadway, and the end effect is lifeless. Manners hated Hollywood, but both it and the film delighted his wife; her biographer even implies a romantic attachment between Vidor and the star. At parties in New York, she would often run the film, leading Ethel Barrymore to answer a dinner invitation with "Miss Barrymore accepts with pleasure if she is assured she will not have to sit through *Peg o' my Heart* again."

The following year, Vidor also directed Miss Taylor in another of her husband's plays, *Happiness*, in which she adapted more comfortably to screen acting. Her mannerisms are subdued in the story of a New York shop girl charming everyone with her optimism. Vidor's obvious sympathy for the film's message encouraged a more personal approach. Even the *New York Times* grudgingly agreed that "this is a photoplay which may teach many to be happy and ambitious." Miss Taylor was less happy, her biographer claims. "There had not been the same fun as with *Peg*. King had fallen in love with Eleanor Boardman and Laurette could never quite forgive one of her 'crushes' for falling in love with somebody else." Her last film for MGM, *One Night in Rome* (1924), was handled by Clarence Badger.

The Taylor films made money and gave Mayer the kudos he wanted. As a reward, Vidor was entrusted with the studio's biggest star, Clara Kimball Young, in a melodrama, *The Woman of Bronze* (1923), which threatened to return him to the artificiality of his films with Florence Vidor. He was delighted when a chance meeting with Major Edward Bowes, then a board member of Samuel Goldwyn Productions, led to an offer to join the company.

A search for artistic respectability obsessed Hollywood in the early twenties as the filmmakers sought justification of their new wealth and influence. European masterpieces, followed in time by their makers, were imposed on an indifferent audience, and distinguished literary figures from both America and Europe were imported to add "tone" to the movies. Jesse Lasky led this abortive quest; at one point, Famous Players-Lasky had more than $8 million tied up in story rights to plays and novels often quite unsuited to film. But Sam Goldwyn was not far behind. A lifelong belief in literary scripts as the basis of film success led him to form Eminent Authors Inc. in 1919 to bring such writers as Rex Beach, Rupert Hughes and Mary Roberts Rinehart to the movies (and at one point to hire six stage and screen critics from New York to advise his filmmakers, a disastrous experiment).

Vidor and Goldwyn fought for the next forty years over the right of the director to write his own scripts, Vidor even submitting a script under an assumed name to prove that a director was as good a scenarist as any New York playwright, but in 1923 the prospect of working with prestigious properties like Austin Strong's *Three Wise Fools* seduced him. He attacked with relish the story of three old bachelors who befriend a young girl and, in time, save her daughter, and almost everyone in the cast — Claude Gillingwater, William Haines, Creighton Hale, Raymond Hatton and Zasu Pitts — went on to fame in the late silent cinema. The film also gave the opportunity to work for the first time with the woman he loved, petite, sharp-featured Eleanor Boardman, then best known as a photographic model but soon to be a major star. As soon as he was divorced from Florence in 1926, Vidor and Eleanor Boardman were married in a ceremony held at Marion Davies' house in Beverly Hills.

Goldwyn's literary acquisitions included some stories by Joseph Hergesheimer, whose *Tol'able David* first attracted Griffith and finally became a hit for Henry King. Goldwyn produced Hergesheimer's *Cythera* in 1924, the same year that Vidor made his film of the same author's *Wild Oranges*. Of all his early films, this Southern melodrama is the most remarkable, and the first to deserve comparison with his work of the forties and fifties. Mayer had offered him the direction of *Ben Hur* at the same time, and though Vidor attributed his refusal to a deep-rooted disbelief in the book's plot, the attractions of Hergesheimer's story must have been influential. Set on a swampy island off the Georgia coast, it shows nature as a sinister force overshadowing the lives of the four people trapped there by an escaped murderer. The wind plays a quirky role, blowing a newspaper across the road to cause the death of the hero's wife by making her horse rear, setting a rocking chair stirring eerily as he enters the house to rescue the girl and her father from the killer, terrifying him by making a shingle flap noisily. The scene in which the slow-thinking but enormously strong murderer carries Virginia Valli through the swamp and maroons her on a tree stump surrounded by mud and alligators presages Vidor's fascination with the swamp as a primeval landscape with its own laws, all of them inimical to man.

After *Happiness*, Vidor was absorbed, like many Mayer employees, into the newly formed Metro-Goldwyn-Mayer, for whom he was to work consistently for the next twenty years. In 1924, MGM had not yet developed the style of high-gloss light dramas and romances that were the basis of its thirties' appeal, but the emphasis on writers which dominated Goldwyn carried through to the new company even though Goldwyn had no official connection with it. Vidor found himself directing *Wine of Youth* (1924), one of the earliest "flapper" romances but sharing the same "east west/home's best" philosophy of the Florence Vidor films. Marjorie Rosen in *Popcorn Venus* remarked that the film "appears to straddle the moral fence but ultimately opts for time-honored virtues. In a lighthearted prologue Vidor sets up a comparison between girls of the twenties and their mothers and grandmothers; these last two we see in flashbacks, sitting on the family's Victorian sofa with their fiances, swooning delicately, 'There's never been so great a love as ours.' Then we meet the liberated flapper Mary, who can't decide which of two beaux to marry, her lively friend Tish, and their boy friends. The two and a half couples propose a camping trip as a 'trial honeymoon' in order to know . . . 'how a man is in everyday life before you give him your all.' Despite provocative, even obligatory flapper sequences — a wild party and the abortive coed camping trip — our 'liberated' daughter resists compromise and ends by snuggling up to her man on the family sofa, murmuring 'There's never been so great a love as ours.' "

As a reliable staff artist, Vidor directed most of MGM's rising stars, including John Gilbert in *His Hour* (1924) from an Elinor Glyn original, and *Wife of the Centaur* (1925), an equally fevered romance whose hero imagines himself the reincarnation of a creature from Greek mythology. Cyril Hume's hectic prose, regarded at the time as highly erotic, was transformed, by all accounts, into a routine film, though Gilbert's moist spaniel eyes and intense style were already earning their soon-to-be international following. Eleanor Boardman, who had starred as Mary in *Wine of Youth* and appeared opposite Gilbert in *Wife of the Centaur*, also starred in

Proud Flesh (1925), a comedy romance about a Californian girl brought up in Spain who returns to upstage her unpolished relatives before succumbing to the pragmatism of a young American bathtub manufacturer.

His Hour, one of the few films to have survived from this period in Vidor's career, transcends its overheated original entirely through a flood of incidents; if you are bored, wait a minute. Gilbert plays the Russian aristocrat Prince Gritzko as if every moment was to be his last, busily organizing a wild party for his Grand Duke (one of Hollywood's many exiled Russian nobles played this role under a pseudonym), only to break it up by letting loose two tigers among the guests. A duel is fought with pistols in a darkened room, the action illuminated by flashes much as Vidor used lightning in many other films. Gilbert is at his best in the febrile scenes of romance in which Miss Glyn specialized; on the set every moment of the shooting, she suggested, among other innovations, a scene in which Gilbert "kissed" Aileen Pringle's cheek with his eyelashes. Though shot, the incident was later removed. (To do justice to her script, Gilbert dressed and ate Russian style throughout the production, and even used a balalaika orchestra to supply mood music during his many private seductions.) In love with the stately Aileen Pringle, he enters her sleeping compartment on a train, briefly nuzzles her hand hanging from the upper berth, then snips a lock of her hair. Later, isolated with the prince in a snowbound dacha after a wild troika ride snuggled up with Gritzko in a fur rug, she averts what she imagines to be inevitable rape by putting a Luger to her head and remaining bolt upright all night, threatening suicide if he assaults her. When, after her collapse, he unbuttons her bodice to search for a pulse, she regards the evidence of her mild deshabille as a pressing argument for their immediate marriage.

Few of these films show Vidor at full stretch, and though he was often able to introduce a dramatically highlighted use of nature, they are not representative of his best work. In any event, his days of servitude as a contract director were soon to be ended by a production which, for all its faults, had a major impact on Hollywood and the cinema of the time, *The Big Parade*.

AN END TO EPHEMERA:

THE BIG PARADE TO SHOW PEOPLE

The Big Parade (1925) changed Vidor's career. From a staff director subject to the studio's whims he became overnight a valued artist able to choose his subjects and stars, courted by actors anxious to share his highbrow status. The film's popularity was as much a surprise to Vidor as it was to MGM, and though he was drawn at the time into making extravagant statements about its qualities — "The human comedy emerges from a terrifying tragedy. The poetry and the romance, the atmosphere, the rhythm and the tempo all find their proper place" — today he recognizes, as many did at the time, that *The Big Parade* is essentially escapist. "I saw it again recently," he said in 1974, "(and) I don't like it much. . . . Today I don't encourage people to see the film. At the time I really believed it was an anti-war movie. Today, if I had to remake it, I would be more precise."

Such rejection is perhaps too sweeping; the film has many striking qualities and adheres well enough to the aims Vidor laid out at the time, before the ballyhoo had reached its climax. Not so much against war as indifferent to it, he wrote, "War is a very human thing, and in the ten years' perspective the human values take prominence and the rest sinks into insignificance. We see the story

Filming of **The Big Parade**

Tom O'Brien, John Gilbert, and Karl Dane in **The Big Parade**

of the individual rather than the mass. We share the heartbeats of the doughboy, his girl and the parents of the two, not ignoring the huge surrounding spectacle but viewing it through the young fighter's eyes. . . . I do not wish to appear as taking any stand about war. I certainly do not favor it but I would not set up a preachment against it."

There is some confusion as to how *The Big Parade* came to be made, but none over the fact that it was not originally intended to be a major ($245,000) production. Vidor says he complained to Irving Thalberg of the "ephemeral films" he was forced to make and suggested such universal topics as wheat, steel, and war. Thalberg told him to look for a suitable war story. *The Big Parade* — title and story both — were based, Vidor recalls, on a five page synopsis submitted by Laurence Stallings, a New York journalist and literary columnist who had lost his right leg at Belleau Wood. His autobiographical novel *Plumes*, published in 1924, skipped the war entirely, expressing instead the exhaustion and disgust of many returning veterans at the indifference of the public to the horror of mutilation and warfare in general. The book ends with the invalid hero attending with his family the interment of the Unknown Soldier; when the man's son, staring into the marble-sided grave, asks with a shudder who puts men into such an awful place, Richard Plume replies, "The general."

"What's a general?"

"A man who makes little boys sleep in graves."

But some of his experiences on the Western front, popularized and given a comic twist, were the basis of *What Price Glory?*, the 1924 play he wrote with Maxwell Anderson. Broadway audiences loved the back-chat between Captain Flagg and Sergeant Quirt, old adversaries who battle over a French saloon girl, and were delightedly shocked by the profanity and fashionable cynicism about war. William Fox snapped up the film rights and Raoul Walsh directed the film in 1926. Thalberg, then on a buying trip to New York, had to be content with the film rights to *Plumes*, and the synopsis offered to Vidor by Stallings when he stepped off the train in California some weeks later represented the logical prologue to his book, showing the young man being swept along by patriotic fervor — "What a thing is patriotism" reads a title; "We go for years not knowing that we love it" — enlisting in the Army and learning to enjoy the company of his comrades in France, as well as the love of a young French girl, Melisande. Returning home after having been crippled, he is resigned to marrying his fiancée, but fortuitously she now loves his brother; he and Melisande are reunited in the glow of a Millet sunset.

Inevitably, Stallings and Vidor romanticized the character of Southern gentleman Jim Apperson (John Gilbert) and the war in which he is changed. Gilbert may, as Vidor suggests, have worn no make-up in the film and dressed only in ill-fitting clothes, but he still looks like an *Esquire* fashion-plate, while Renée Adorée as the girl is, one French critic bitingly remarked, "dressed like a burlesque miller's wife." Even Vidor acknowledged that the famous scene where she is left behind by the departing army, clutching only his old boot, was played "to jerk a tear," and the comedy between Gilbert, Tom O'Brien and the tobacco-spitting Karl Dane recalls the appeal to the stalls of *What Price Glory?* Shrewdly, Vidor shot first the film's most dramatic sequence in which Apperson, trapped in No Man's Land, gropes his way by shell flashes to a crater where a German soldier is dying in the mud. Impressed by the rushes, Thalberg decided to make *The Big Parade* a "feature picture," and the Army was called in to plan lavish scenes of troops marching across France. Later, when the film was finished, J. J. McCarthy, the exhibitor whose splash release of *Ben Hur* was to make that film MGM's other big hit of 1926, offered to do the same for *The Big Parade* if more romance was added and the battle scenes were given greater impact. Vidor obligingly provided the fiancée sub-plot and action specialist George Hill the battles. It went on to gross $18 million, showing Thalberg's extraordinary instinct for a commercial product. Louis B. Mayer never lost his dislike of the film. Six years later, George S. Kaufman reported, he was still complaining that Vidor had shown a toilet in one scene, which he regarded as "a terrible lapse of good taste."

Stripped of MGM's publicity and the spurious anti-war sentiment, *The Big Parade* emerges as a creditable John Gilbert romantic vehicle, with many decorative elements familiar from Vidor's

Renée Adorée and Gilbert in **The Big Parade**

other work. The soft-focus rural idylls, the scenes of the army winding across the hills of France or advancing through a shaded wood (as a young man, Vidor shot documentary footage of the US Army on maneuvers in Texas, re-using some of the same compositions for this film) are heavily romanticized; even the shell holes in the farmhouse were painted on to avoid unintentional glimpses of the MGM backlot. The war scenes are brief, and follow the long love story in which Miss Adorée, despite her absurd costume, makes an impression of charm and sensuality. One's objections to *The Big Parade* are less to the film itself than to its false reputation; as a glamorized picture of war, it compares favorably with *Hearts of the World, Pilgrimage* and other war romances of the time.

Friends of Laurence Stallings contest Vidor's version of events. "Stallings wrote the story, and was allowed to select the director and the most important stars," said Robert E. Sherwood, a friend of Stallings from the Algonquin Round Table, when reviewing the film. Stallings, he went on, called Hollywood people "dim wits," and he did insist that Vidor and co-scenarist Harry Behn come east to write the script away from California's pernicious influence. Like many writers who earned their reputation with war-based material, Stallings did not live up to his early promise. Four more plays with Anderson did poorly, and he settled down as editor of Fox Movietone Newsreels and a Hollywood screenwriter, particularly for Vidor, for whom he worked on *Show People, Billy the Kid, So Red the Rose, Northwest Passage* and *A Miracle Can Happen*. None, however, achieved the fame of *The Big Parade*.

Thalberg confirmed MGM's view of *The Big Parade* as a Gilbert vehicle by allocating the same star to Vidor for his next two films, a big budget version of *La Bohème* (1926) to star Gilbert and the studio's newest acquisition, Lillian Gish, and *Bardelys the Magnificent* (1926), in which he romped with unaccustomed panache in a story adapted from Rafael Sabatini. Little seen today, *La Bohème* has great and enduring merit, containing one of Lillian Gish's most intense performances. With the honeymoon period of her contract still at its height, she could dictate terms to Thalberg. As a subject she asked for a version of Murger's *Scenes de la vie de Bohème* adapted by her friend Mme. Frederick de Gresac, and for her di-

Lillian Gish and Karl Dane in ***La Bohème***

rector, after seeing two reels of the still-uncompleted *The Big Parade*, King Vidor. Even Vidor's reverence for Griffith flagged when Miss Gish demanded full rehearsals in The Master's style, but like all her directors he could not fault her dedication. Preparing to play the frail seamstress Mimi who sacrifices herself so that her lover, the playwright Rodolphe, can write his masterpiece, she visited hospitals to study the symptoms of terminal tuberculosis, drank no fluids for three days before her death scene and dried her mouth with cotton pads. This sequence — actually quite routine in effect, though cast and crew found it traumatic — is merely the culmination of a performance disturbing in its sense of sickness. The feeling of cold as she huddles in her unfloored and empty flat, the blood-smeared mouth after her first seizure, her exhaustion as she drags herself like a sick cat across Paris, clinging to passing vehicles and to the vast city walls as Paris towers indifferently above her are components of a rich, moving characterization beside which Gilbert's capering Rodolphe and the other bohemians, no matter how Vidor makes them dance, clown and pose to enliven the static script, become irrelevant.

La Bohème showed Gilbert in a poor light — literally, since Miss Gish brought in Hendrick Sartov to create glamorized, heavily gauzed close-ups that undermined his importance to the story. (Erté had also been hired to do the costumes; the star rejected his designs as too fancy.) Gilbert, according to Miss Gish, fell in love with her and proposed marriage when the film ended, so he may have been happy to give her the lioness's share of the production. He was no better served by *Bardelys the Magnificent*. With Gilbert's collusion and perhaps with covert encouragement from Mayer, who disliked his amoral life style and sensed that the era of the matinee idol was dying, Vidor used Sabatini's story to show Gilbert in a new and unflattering light, that of an action star *à la* Douglas Fairbanks. Cutting a poor figure as a fencer and relying on stunt men for such spectacular coups as an escape from his own execution on a parachute improvised from an awning, Gilbert is comfortable only in the love scenes, particularly the much-quoted river sequence in which he and Eleanor Boardman glide under drooping willow boughs. Despite the efforts of many close friends, including Vidor, Gilbert destroyed himself with drink and melancholy, both the actor and the industry magnifying the problems of his light speaking voice into an obsession. "Jack died before his time," said Vidor, "and death perhaps came as a great relief."

Gilbert and Gish in **La Bohème**

For all their elegance and flair, *La Bohème* and *Bardelys the Magnificent* could have been the work of any top MGM staff director; Clarence Brown might well have extracted more from them than did Vidor. But Vidor, like Griffith, regarded himself as a thinker on film. Now established at Metro, he could enlarge on his personal ethic, exhort audiences to optimism and self-help, and offer cautionary tales on the perils of failure. One might have expected films which mined the same profitable vein as Frank Capra's, but Vidor's pragmatism, characteristic of one brought up in Christian Science, ensured that his parables were underlaid with a bleak doubt. While Ford and Capra knew that a good man who kept faith would always survive, Vidor believed that survival is subject to the caprice of a malevolent destiny. As Job meditates, the Lord giveth, but the Lord taketh away. This is the message of his most unusual and uncharacteristic film of the twenties, *The Crowd* (1928).

In 1928, German filmmakers enjoyed an American vogue with the studio owners if not with the public. The artistic success of *The Last Laugh, The Street, Metropolis, Asphalt, Backstairs* and *Variety* earned Hollywood contracts for Murnau, May, Leni and Dupont. None had happy Hollywood careers but their influence was at its peak just before sound, with William Fox basking in the *succès d'estime* of *Sunrise,* directed by his "German genius" F. W. Murnau. Films like *Sunrise* replaced the romantic image of urban life with that of The City, impersonal and characterless. Like the books of Norris, Dos Passos and Sinclair Lewis, "City films" emphasized the rhythm imposed by work, showing crowds sucked into office buildings each morning and spewed out at night. Most had sequences set in places of mass entertainment where people were shown as regimented at play as they were at work, and in each the city finally destroys all illusions, reducing everyone to the same dreary norm.

The Crowd mocks the Horatio Alger fiction of the self-improving young American. Vidor had claimed to be making "The Big Parade of Peace," but it is only in its hero, feckless, ebullient but slow John Sims (James Murray) that *The Crowd* has any affinities with that romantic work. Born on the 4th July, 1900 — "America's 124th Birthday," a title notes — he is greeted by a proud father as "a little man the world's going to hear from" but the film relentlessly points out that we are all marked by social and racial stereotypes from birth. As the children discuss their future jobs (the black boy says "I detend to be a preacher-man. Hallelujah!") John finds his future blighted by his father's sudden death. In a dramatic use of Expressionist forced perspective, a stairway opens out, with the crowd huddled below and John standing, baffled and confused, half-way between his ruined past and an unknown future. Helpless in New York — "You've got to be good in that town if you want to beat the crowd," a gaunt stranger remarks bitterly as they stare at the skyline from a ferry — he is soon reduced to a number in a characterless office. He proposes to his girl on a trip

Forced perspective in ***The Crowd***

Eleanor Boardman and James Murray in ***The Crowd***

to Coney Island, they honeymoon in Niagara Falls — the love scene by Niagara's cataract is a lonely example in the film of Vidor's erotic fascination with nature — and despite the windfall of a $500 slogan contest prize, The City robs them of their youth, their optimism and even one of their children, killed by a truck as she runs to receive presents bought with the money. The crowd is indifferent to suffering.

"The world can't stop just because your baby's ill," says a cop as John tries to quiet the passers-by under his window, and when she dies their grief is equally ephemeral. "The crowd laughs with you always, but it will cry with you for only a day." Unable to forget her death, John loses his job and is drawn down through a series of demeaning positions until, Mary having been persuaded by her family to leave him, he contemplates suicide, but is too scared to jump under the train. His son's affection encourages him to take a job as a juggling sandwich-board man (a recurring figure, reminiscent of the blind man and the clown in *M* and *The Blue Angel*, whom they mock earlier with the remark "I bet his father expected him to be President") and when he returns home Mary decides to remain. Seven endings to this bleak parable were shot, ranging from a sentimental tableau in which John, an overnight success in advertising, celebrates an affluent Christmas with the family, to that most commonly used; John and Mary visit a vaudeville show with their son and laugh at two tumbling clowns until the camera cranes up to show them melting once more into the mindlessly laughing crowd.

The Crowd has some affinities with the simplistic *Love Never Dies*, but its real resemblance is to the fatalistic and impersonal films of a Europe haunted by the specter of social inequality. Much of the film's character flows from its star James Murray, a minor actor (Vidor incorrectly describes him as an "extra"; he had actually played featured roles since 1923) who, though no better than routine in his intense sequences with Eleanor Boardman, catches exactly the right tone in the film's lighter moments. As the ukelele-strumming, wise-cracking young husband taking the family to the beach and watching complacently while his wife cooks lunch and fights with the kids, or the self-pitying vacuum cleaner salesman saying listlessly "I don't suppose you'd want one of these, would you?" to the hundredth uninterested housewife in the hundredth identical house, he personifies in one character the cruel deception of the American dream. There is a grim appropriateness in the fact that Murray's career never took off, despite the success of *The Crowd*. His acting work became sporadic and in 1936, apparently drunk and out of work, he fell into the Hudson River and drowned. "When he fell the people watching thought it was a gag," said Vidor. "He was always gagging. Then he floated up and it was too late."

Murray in ***The Crowd***

Not released for a year because of its gloomy theme, *The Crowd* drew approving reviews and a modest profit, but could not hope to equal *The Big Parade* in either kudos or income. Vidor, who had rashly signed away his percentage of *The Big Parade* at the behest of a fast-talking MGM lawyer, was still a contract director and, always aware of the need to keep working, even on minor films, to keep one's name alive, he may have been grateful for the interest shown in his career by newspaper magnate William Randoph Hearst who, in the conviction that only the best was good enough for his mistress Marion Davies, insisted that the maker of *The Big Parade* handle her next films now that Cosmopolitan Pictures, his puppet corporation devoted to her screen career, had set up its headquarters on the MGM lot.

His ability as a comedy director confirmed by the two Laurette Taylor films, Vidor did a professional job with Davies on *The Patsy* (1928), *Show People* (1928) and *Not So Dumb* (1930). The last, an

Marion Davies and Marie Dressler in **The Patsy**

adaptation of the hit play *Dulcy* by Marc Connelly and George S. Kaufman, was released as Vidor's second sound film after *Hallelujah!* and exposed the thinness of Miss Davies' talent, but the first two, in which, freed of the necessity to deliver lines, she could exhibit her vivacity and knack for imitation and parody, are delightful. Reflecting her true nature as a feather-headed party girl who liked to clown and send up her friends, both cast her as a charming but selfish girl determined to get what she wanted, even at the expense of others. In *The Patsy* she sets her cap for her sister's boyfriend, and after a series of ploys — including a display of her "personality" in which she does passable imitations of Negri, Gish and Mae Murray — gets him in the end. *Show People,* based on a play called "Polly Preferred" which Vidor "couldn't even bear to read all the way through," cast her as Peggy Pepper, a southern actress who, after breaking into movies with slapstick comedy, becomes a serious star, marries a French count and, as "Peggy Pepoire," queens it over Hollywood.

Vidor had no difficulty finding major stars to play comic bits — "It was a Hearst film. They didn't dare refuse" — so John Gilbert, Mae Murray, Douglas Fairbanks, Elinor Glyn, Lew Cody, as well as

Davies imitating Swanson, Gish, and Murray for Vidor during making of ***The Patsy***

*Davies and William Haines in **Show People***

his regular collaborators Aileen Pringle, Karl Dane and George K. Arthur all appear as themselves, as does Davies, a double exposure figure in tennis clothes with whom Peggy claims to be unimpressed. Chaplin has the film's best moment when Peggy graciously offers him her autograph. In both films, Vidor shrewdly backed Davies with polished professionals; Dell Henderson and Marie Dressler played her parents in *The Patsy*, while Ralph Spence, Hollywood's top title writer, gave the films their best comic lines: "Your mother has her good points, Pat," says Henderson in *The Patsy*. "She sure has," Marion snaps. "They stick out all over her."

Although Vidor says he based Peggy on Gloria Swanson, with whose life there are some resemblances, the tone is more personal and, on occasions bitter, suggesting that Florence Vidor may be the subject. Like Florence, Peggy comes by car from Georgia with a man who has promised to get her into films (in this case her father), she takes early jobs in comedies, — Hearst refused to show Marion hit with a custard pie, so a soda siphon was used — and graduates to tear-jerking dramas in which her emotions have to be encouraged with mood music and onions. When she becomes a top star, the ultimate accolade is to be directed by King Vidor, who is seen working on both *The Big Parade* and *Bardelys the Magnificent*.

Haines, Davies, and Chaplin in **Show People**

A VOICE FOR THE DEVIL:
THE SOUND FILMS

Unlike some other directors of the Griffith school — Henry King, Marshall Neilan, James Cruze — Vidor adapted well to sound. Dialogue never interested him a lot, but as an amateur musician — banjo and guitar — the opportunity to heighten an effect with music or sound effects gave him a particular pleasure. Now he could give a voice to the devil he saw in nature. Characteristically it was one which hummed with violence and a covert sexuality. His growing reputation also gave him the confidence to abandon the stage-bound approach of his late silent period, a change hastened by the growth of a strong American documentary tradition. "I was developing a style that could integrate the seemingly disparate styles I had worked with before, the dramatic, entertaining story line with the realism and credibility of a Flaherty-type documentary. I had either consciously or unconsciously been moving in this direction from the start."

Hallelujah, his first sound film, dramatized the pitfalls of this approach. So convincing are the scenes of black life in the South, shot around Memphis, Tennessee, that footage of cotton-picking and the loading of a river boat from lines of bale-laden wagons have been mistaken for newsreel and used in compilation films.

Hallelujah

The mass baptism in the river and many scenes set in the black shanty town are equally realistic, with little attempt at fantasy. They contrast markedly with the film's dramatic plot, a triangle melodrama culminating in a cuckolded preacher pursuing his wife's lover through a swamp. Northern blacks hooted the film, which Vidor attributed to the fact that "the Harlem Negro does not know his southern brother as he is so far removed, and as the Northerner is so intent on being like the white man." He also suggested that "the laughter might have been caused by the Negro's merriment at tragedy," a grotesque thesis soon dropped. "Everything (in the film) I had seen when I was a child," he said. "I remember that there was a black woman in my family. I made this film for her. I should have dedicated it to her." But inevitably it reflects, like Griffith's films, a now-disconcerting paternalism. "I am a Southerner and believe I know Negroes better than the average film director," Vidor said at the time. His vision of the black as a mindless hedonist singing the day away may be specious, but it is of its time. Vidor's contribution to the film is a freshness of technique, a delight in the use of natural sound and a sense of animal vitality in his people. Above all, he celebrates the landscape as one people use, live in and, at moments of tension, are subject to. The pursuit of the fleeing lover through the swamp amid bird cries and the predatory sucking of the mud is one of the most impressive sequences in all his work.

With *Hallelujah*, Vidor extended his sense of nature as a malevolent force to show industry as man's most potent attempt to subdue the earth. Cotton is a continuous presence, and its harvest and shipping a major preoccupation. Later films emphasize industry even more; *The Citadel* (coal), *An American Romance* (steel), *Our Daily Bread* (wheat), *Duel in the Sun* (cattle, the railroad), *The Fountainhead* (construction), *Beyond the Forest* (lumber) and *Japanese War Bride* (truck farming). But all show industry as a battle between man and nature which man can only win by sacrificing part of himself.

For Vidor, the early sound period was a time of redefinition. Initially irritated by the stampede to talkies just as silent cinema was being perfected, he adjusted well and, with *Hallelujah*, made one of the most audacious early sound films. But MGM protested when he pointed out that many genres would now no longer survive in the old form. Hemingway, whom Vidor met on a 1928 Paris trip, pioneered a terse and colloquial dialogue style, which Vidor unsuccessfully attempted to imitate in his similar clipped realistic lines in *Not So Dumb* (1930). The chatty Kaufman/Connelly play was hardly the right vehicle for such an experiment; Vidor acknowledged, "realism or not, it didn't hold the attention," and removed the scenes. As the tactless daughter of a house-party hostess given to disastrous malapropisms and gaffes, Davies lacks

Davies and Donald Ogden Stewart in ***Not So Dumb***

the snap such dialogue needs. She is saved by the skill of her supporting players; Franklin Pangborn as a wordy old-style scenario writer and New York wit Donald Ogden Stewart as a golf-obsessed imposter who has most of the film's best quips.

But both Vidor and Laurence Stallings felt a Western might lend itself to this new approach. The clichés of frontier film had begun to ring false even in the form of silent titles and, as he remarked at the time, "speech revealed these old time situations in no flattering light." After a long argument with MGM, *Billy the Kid* (1930) went before the cameras two years after Vidor and Stallings submitted the idea, and proved to be one of the most arresting of early sound Westerns, dignified by the brevity and realism Hemingway had pioneered. Billy and Pat Garrett, played by ex-football star Johnny Mack Brown and Wallace Beery, are intruders in an implacable landscape of stone, sand and scrub where conversation means nothing. Men die badly, coughing blood, or crawl to hide in caves so huge that they mock man and his conceits. MGM decided to sell the film as an epic by shooting it in the 70mm Realife Grandeur system, reducing it to 35mm for other theatres. With only a few cinemas capable of showing 70mm its epic quality and Grand Canyon locations were wasted.

Delusions of grandeur also inhibited *Street Scene* (1931). Confined to one set, the street in front of a crowded tenement, Elmer Rice's play exposed the violence that breeds in the frustration and congestion of city life. A deserted wife and her children are turned out for non-payment of rent, a young and sensitive Jew is mocked by his neighbors, a woman, driven to adultery by the indifference

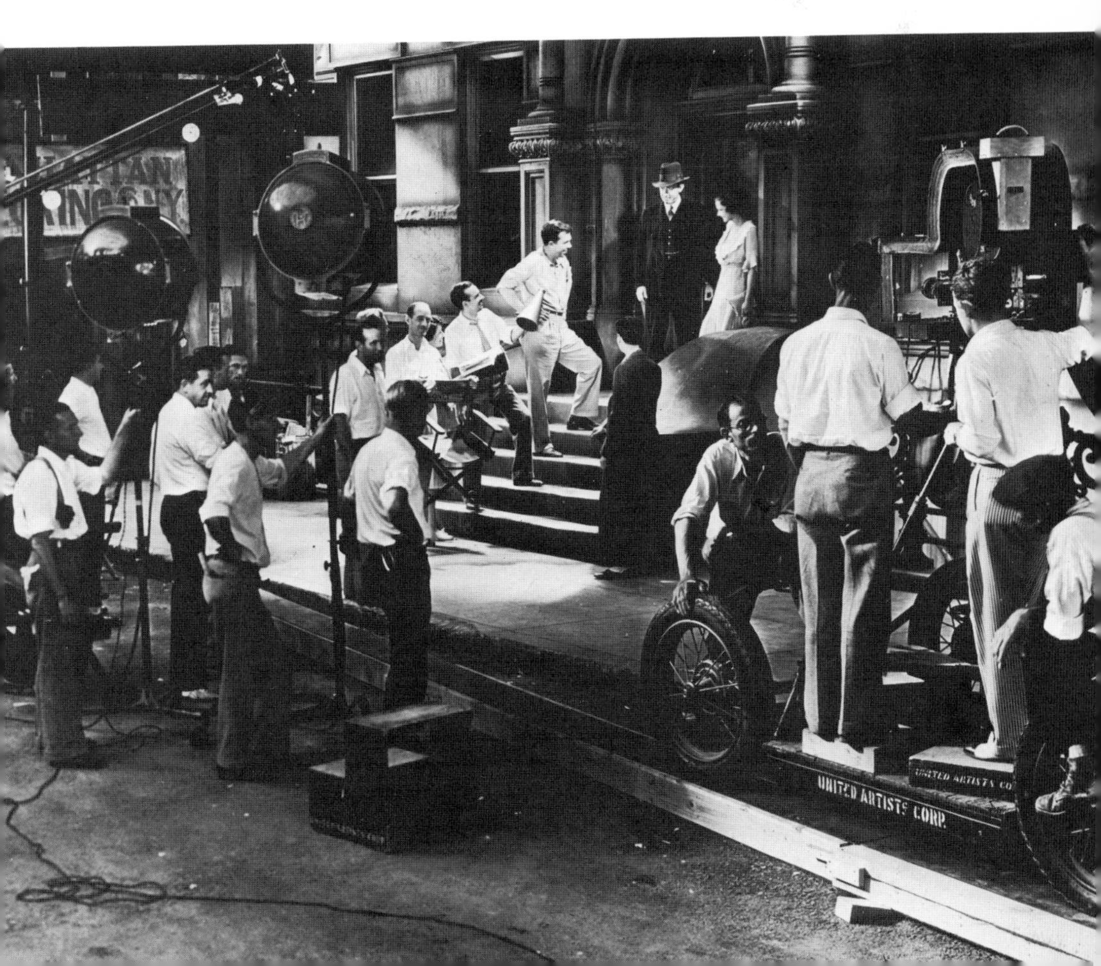

Filming of ***Street Scene***

of her husband, is murdered with her lover, and the dead woman's daughter becomes the mistress of a rich man to survive. By focusing on a single organism in the city, Rice exposed the universal blight of social inequality, but it is typical of Sam Goldwyn's approach — Vidor made the film on loan-out from MGM — that an entire city block, including elevated railway tracks, a drug store and a number of houses were built for the film, and Alfred Newman commissioned to write a music score (one of his most successful, its theme was re-used frequently over the next thirty years). With the play's leftist ideology blunted by the censorship of many lines spoken by the young Jew and the old Communist, and the realistic material betrayed by heavily theatrical acting from Estelle Taylor (though Sylvia Sidney as the young girl and Beulah Bondi as a gossiping resident are excellent), *Street Scene* betrayed its original as Goldwyn was to similarly betray *Dead End* five years later. Vidor agreed with the changes and enjoyed the technical challenge of sending his camera craning through his huge set; an urban romantic, he is a political and social innocent.

The Champ (1931), a sentimental vehicle for Wallace Beery as a decayed boxer with Jackie Cooper as his son, has few recognizable Vidor touches, but *Bird of Paradise* (1932), a classic South Seas triangle story — boy, girl, volcano — made on location in Hawaii for David Selznick, to whose RKO Vidor was briefly on loan, does have its bizarre place in his canon, if only for its eroticism. Shooting without a script and racing the deadlines of other films for its stars, Joel McCrea and Dolores Del Rio, Vidor shot mainly documentary footage of natives rowing out to greet a visiting yacht, McCrea posing half-naked against palm-fringed skylines and Miss Del Rio romping through the jungle in a grass skirt and brief but immovable lei. Saved from a shark by Princess Luana (Del Rio), a favor for which he repays her, after an explicit nude swim, by initiating her into the Western ritual of the kiss, Johnny (McCrea) lands on the beach with a few necessities of life, then electrifies the natives by batting flying fish out of the air with a tennis racquet, trading news of Luana's whereabouts for a phonograph that plays "The Darktown Strutter's Ball," and carrying her off in a canoe fitted with an outboard motor.

Wallace Beery and Jackie Cooper in **The Champ**

Back in Hollywood, Vidor added the native dance sequences (choreographed by an uncredited Busby Berkeley) and confected a plot in which Del Rio tearfully renounces McCrea in favor of her duty to placate the volcano by leaping into its crater. *Bird of Para-*

dise has arresting examples of pre-Breen Office eroticism, with its nude swimming, a sadistic scene of the lovers hanging from bamboo poles and trying to kiss, and Del Rio sucking an orange, then transferring the juice to McCrea's fevered mouth. Perhaps significantly, Vidor fell in love with his script girl Elizabeth Hill during the making of the film. He and Eleanor Boardman were divorced in 1932, and he and Miss Hill married shortly after.

Again on loan to Goldwyn, Vidor made *Cynara* (1932), a stolid melodrama dignified by a fine Ronald Colman performance as an upright English lawyer whose happy but boring marriage is interrupted by an affair with a young girl whose suicide ruins both marriage and career. Colman's decency and good humor never fail throughout the affair, however much he may dislike his mistress's shop-girl manners. The triumph of his performance and Vidor's direction is that he makes the lapse seem more one of good taste

Dolores Del Rio and Joel McCrea in ***Bird of Paradise***

Phyllis Barry and Ronald Colman in **Cynara**

than of morals, for which his wife (Kay Francis) in the end graciously forgives him as he sets out to make a new life in Africa. The same theme was to reappear in Vidor's version of Marquand's *H.M. Pulham Esq.* in 1941, where interior monologue makes the conflict even more effective.

MGM's persistent error of typing directors also afflicted Vidor, who found his interest in rural subjects used against him in a series of opulent country melodramas where his simplistic, instinctive sense of the land and its spiritual significance was debased by big budgets and stars. *The Stranger's Return* (1933), *The Wedding*

Night (1935) and *So Red the Rose* (1935) are choked in lush greenery, nodding flowers and rolling green hills, in contrast to the cheaper *Wild Oranges* and *Japanese War Bride*, where economy of resources was echoed in a sparse clarity. Of these rural films, *The Stranger's Return* excels. The stranger is Miriam Hopkins, a city girl who returns to the Iowa farm of her patriarchal grandfather (played with relish by Lionel Barrymore in a rehearsal for his Wagnerian Senator McCanles in *Duel in the Sun*) and learns the reverence for the soil forgotten by his other relatives in their greed for the land. Vidor renders the sentimentality of Phil Stong's novel with more restraint than did Henry King in his version of the same author's *State Fair*, with an emphasis on rural ritual and a love of the landscape, but the absence of a sinister undercurrent finally robs the film of a necessary intensity.

Vidor's next film, *Our Daily Bread* (1934), stands as high in his estimation as *The Crowd*, though it is not surprising that Thalberg, who had encouraged Vidor in his reaction against "ephemeral films," was uninterested in this "wheat" section of his "war, wheat

Our Daily Bread

and steel" trilogy; a film in which the young couple of *The Crowd* inherit a farm in the depth of the Depression and make it pay by harnessing the unemployed was hardly what MGM needed in a period of national optimism and growing prosperity. Naive and simplistic — the idea, significantly, was suggested by an article in *The Reader's Digest* — *Our Daily Bread* redeemed itself by Vidor's sincerity and a charming performance by Karen Morley as the wife. The film's set pieces, particularly the climax in which John, fleeing his crumbling commune with a corrupt city girl, finds a hidden stream and leads the workers in improvising an irrigation system to water the fields, have dated badly in their solemn mock-Soviet montage. The most durable things are the simplest; Robert Planck's relaxed photography of the rural landscape and the incidental playing of people like Barbara Pepper as the city girl. Forced on Vidor as the price of a backer's participation, she represents with her slovenly sexuality and inevitable gramophone a credible thirties' femme fatale.

Sam Goldwyn's attempt to launch Russian-born Anna Sten as the new Dietrich had become a standing joke in Hollywood by the time Vidor took over *The Wedding Night* (1935). A skillful actress in Europe, she never developed a successful English voice, despite a year's tuition (mainly seeing old Hollywood movies). In an unpublished verse to one of his best-known songs, Cole Porter remarked "If Sam Goldwyn can/With great conviction/Instruct Anna Sten in diction/Then Anna shows/Anything Goes." Goldwyn's efforts reduced the accent but Vidor recalls that her deliberate and measured speech, combined with the laconic delivery of her co-star Gary Cooper, miscast as a wordy novelist (based, Vidor says, on Scott Fitzgerald), made direction an agonizing process. The observation of customs in an immigrant Polish family undercuts the unlikelihood of Cooper's romance with Sten, and the final scenes of her death at the height of a drunken wedding party remain brutally dramatic.

Aided by Gregg Toland's photography — Vidor praised his economy in the use of lights, making set-ups quick and easy — even Cooper's final speech on the death of his lover has a dignified, funereal tone. Almost unaware of his estranged wife in his grief

Anna Sten and Ralph Bellamy in **The Wedding Night**

over the girl's death, Cooper stands by the window and soliloquizes about her vivacity, "She was always so alive to me." Anxious to communicate his vision of the girl to his wife, he turns to find she has slipped away. Only then does the Goldwyn pathos assert itself in a maudlin "reappearance" of Sten running down the hill, a cliché re-used to even worse effect in *Wuthering Heights*.

The late thirties were a trough in Vidor's career. *So Red the Rose* (1935), an old-fashioned film of a Carolina family decaying under the pressure of the Civil War, fell back on the clichés of amiable, simpleton slaves and elegant gentry that *Gone With the Wind* was to redeem with exhiliration and technical panache. Vidor, who claims Stark Young's novel and his film presaged *Gone With the Wind*, long before Margaret Mitchell's book was ever written, was offered the direction of the MGM film, but in pausing

Vidor on location for **The Texas Rangers**

over a weekend to read the book, found himself nudged out by George Cukor. *The Texas Rangers* (1936), a celebration of the Texas Centennial which Vidor was a logical choice to direct, collapsed into a series of Western clichés. Two outlaws (Fred MacMurray and Jack Oakie) respond to hard times by becoming Rangers in the hope of learning how to be better thieves, only to see the light and find themselves hunting an old buddy (Lloyd Nolan) who had flourished on the other side as the Polka Dot Bandit.

Fred MacMurray and Jean Parker in **The Texas Rangers**

Widespread antipathy also greeted *Stella Dallas* (1937), with a miscast Barbara Stanwyck playing the sacrificing mother, the role in which Belle Bennett had made a personal triumph in the 1926 version. Already established as an emancipated heroine in films like *The Bitter Tea of General Yen*, Stanwyck lacked credibility as the social-climbing woman who, like so many Vidor heroines, comes "from the wrong side of the tracks" and sacrifices the thing she loves — in this case, her daughter — so that she can have the happiness of fashionable marriage to a socialite.

In the mid-thirties, the British government moved belatedly to stop the erosion of its film industry by foreign producers, demanding that a large percentage of money earned in its cinemas be ploughed back into local production. The effort would soon enough be reduced to the cranking out of primitive "quota quickies" but MGM, the biggest earner in the country who now found millions of dollars "blocked" there, was anxious to "show willing" and, with some publicity, signed generous contracts for British productions and stars. Among the first actors to sign was Robert Donat, whose deal promised $63,000 a film for six films — the contract was open dated, since Donat was often unable to work because of asthma — the first of them to be A. J. Cronin's *The Citadel*. Despite poor health, Donat gave a good performance as the doctor who develops from a bumbling locum in a Welsh

Robert Donat in ***The Citadel***

Vidor chats with miners during filming of ***The Citadel***

mining village to a Harley Street specialist in the diseases of the rich, then gives it all up to work with a brilliant but unqualified "quack" on the pioneering fringes of medicine. The first half is rich and precise; young Manson peering excitedly from the train as glimpses of mining life reel by, contending with the meanness and ignorance of Welsh village life before colluding with a fellow doctor (gleefully overplayed by Ralph Richardson) to blow up the sewer which causes its chronic diseases. Thereafter, *The Citadel* is only fitfully effective, with Rosalind Russell obviously uncomfortable as his schoolteacher wife, and the detail of a London physician's life sketched with a shabbiness emphasizing the gap between British technique and the skill of Hollywood. Vidor is at his best in the set pieces, notably a mining rescue which dramatizes his fear and awe at the industrial process, but the Academy Award nominations for his direction and the script, by Ian Dalrymple, Frank Wead and his wife, Elizabeth Hill Vidor, were probably political.

MGM's assembly line system caught up even top directors like Vidor, who could be called in to pass judgment on a new property or even prepare a project, only to find themselves a few days later shifted to something else. In the late thirties, Vidor, in addition to being offered *Gone With the Wind,* spent many months on Marjorie Kinnan Rawlings' *The Yearling,* then planned as a Spencer Tracy vehicle. Hundreds of sprouting corn plants were growing in hothouses on the Southern location and a production line of does had been impregnated to ensure that the film's main character, a yearling deer, would not grow older noticeably as the film went on, but the project was destroyed, in an irony the nature-loving Vidor obviously found amusing, when the animals refused to produce replacement offspring out of season. Without a new young deer every week the film could not be shot, so Spencer Tracy was released and *The Yearling,* when it was finally made, starred Gregory Peck under Clarence Brown's direction. One of Vidor's less well publicized jobs at the time was the direction of a section of *The Wizard of Oz* (1939) when director Victor Fleming was unavailable. Vidor found himself handling what is perhaps the film's most famous sequence, Judy Garland singing *Over the Rainbow.*

Although *Northwest Passage* preceded them, two further pictures, *Comrade X* (1940) and *H.M. Pulham Esq.* (1941), belong to the period of indecision that produced *So Red the Rose* and *The Texas Rangers.* Both, like *The Citadel,* were miscast, notably in the use of Hedy Lamarr who, after having been bought by Mayer against his better judgment mainly to forestall offers from other studios, was shuttled from one inappropriate vehicle to another. Her sole artistic success in Hollywood came in *Algiers,* the remake of Duvivier's *Pepe Le Moko* which she did on loan to independent producer Walter Wanger. *Comrade X,* an unashamed self-plagiarism by MGM of its 1939 success *Ninotchka,* sent up Soviet Russia, with Lamarr as a Moscow tram conductor opposite a clearly bored Clark Gable; *Ninotchka*'s Felix Bressart again plays a comic Russian, but with Vladimir Sokoloff and Oscar Homolka replacing Sig Ruman and Alexander Granach. There are good jokes on Russian incompetence — "The lift has been jammed for days."

"Call the repair man."

Vidor with third wife Elizabeth Hill, 1937

Hedy
CLARK
GABLE • LAMARR
Comrade X
THE FUNNIEST
LOVE COMEDY
SINCE
"NINOTCHKA"!
a KING VIDOR
Production
WITH
OSCAR HOMOLKA
FELIX BRESSART
EVE ARDEN
SCREEN PLAY BY BEN HECHT AND CHARLES LEDERER
A METRO-GOLDWYN-MAYER
PICTURE
Directed by
KING VIDOR
Produced by
GOTTFRIED REINHARDT
B

"We think he's in it" — and a comic funeral gives the film some good moments, but in general it is a pale carbon copy. Lamarr's brave attempt at the role of an advertising copywriter in *H.M. Pulham Esq.* is overshadowed by the calm, relaxed playing of Robert Young, whom Vidor called "a superb actor without a single problem." In a series of flashbacks recalling an uneventful life of rectitude and quiet achievement, the film developed a character of dignity and charm, but it is essentially a style Vidor had decided to forget. Between 1939 and 1959 his preoccupation was increasingly to be with nature, industry and vast forces, the stuff on which his best work has always been founded.

THE STOCK MARKET OF THE SPIRIT:

NORTHWEST PASSAGE TO THE FOUNTAINHEAD

The forties and early fifties were Vidor's greatest period. The post-war optimism and MGM's limitless resources brought his romantic imagination to a full, late maturity. This was the time of *An American Romance, The Fountainhead, Duel in the Sun, Beyond the Forest* and *Ruby Gentry* — and, inaugurating the golden age, his adaptation of Kenneth Roberts' *Northwest Passage* (1940), a saga of pre-Revolutionary America and the attempts to open up a fictitious passage to Asia.

If *Duel in the Sun* is most characteristic of this rich period in Vidor's career, then Spencer Tracy, the star of *Northwest Passage*, is its most emblematic actor. "Tracy, along with Robert Donat, just about heads my list of the best actors I've worked with," wrote Vidor. "Everything that Spencer did came over with tremendous conviction." Vidor had expected to direct Tracy in *The Yearling* and also asked him to take the lead in *An American Romance*. One sees what Vidor admired in Tracy, the sense of moral worth and indomitability but as well the sensitivity which exhibited itself personally in Tracy's insecurity and heavy drinking. During location shooting on *Northwest Passage* in Idaho Tracy "repeatedly threatened to leave the location and return to Los Angeles before the

Crossing the river in ***Northwest Passage***

job was finished. I had to use several unusual methods to placate his fears and calm him." Little of this strain shows in the film which, in any event, centers more on the story of a young artist (Robert Young) who joins the group of British Army irregulars led by Captain Rogers to escape the consequences of his anti-British political remarks. The film, which was to have been in two parts — *Northwest Passage* is subtitled "Part One: Rogers' Rangers" — covers only the trek by Rogers to exterminate an Indian tribe which, encouraged by the French, has been raiding settlements. The second section was never made.

Vidor's temptation in his first color film to wallow in visuals of the unspoiled Northwest was considerable, but he readily rejected the merely scenic when opportunities existed to explore his jaded view of landscape. To the Rangers, alone and cut off from

Spencer Tracy and Robert Young with the sketchbook in **Northwest Passage**

their supplies, nature is an enemy which kills many and leaves the rest emaciated, reduced to scavenging and, in one case, cannibalism. The Indians they attack, and whose barbarism is well outlined in the often gruesomely outspoken script by Laurence Stallings and Talbot Jennings, are no more savage than the rivers and swamps they must ford to find them. Standing on a rock addressing his men before the expedition commences, Rogers significantly draws on another rock, suggesting that even the most basic benefits of civilization, such as paper, must be left behind. The survival of Young's sketchbook with its images of a forgotten civilization becomes, as the film develops, a source of wonder. Vidor trained for his excursion into color by taking up painting, and if the film has a fault it is its "painterly" look: Indian canoes outlined against the setting sun, vistas of rolling hills that have a decorative emptiness reminiscent of Sunday watercolor. But Vidor commendably neutralizes the sweetness of the color with documentary realism; in cutting for tension, in evoking the special character of a location and, notably in a scene of portaging boats over a mountain, where he recalls the finale of *Our Daily Bread*. In sheer manipulation of the medium, *Northwest Passage* is unmistakably a master work.

Tracy's success in *Northwest Passage* made his refusal to star in *An American Romance* (1944) even more hurtful to Vidor. Ingrid Bergman and Joseph Cotten, his choices for female lead and second lead, were also unavailable, and he compromised on a cast of Brian Donlevy, Ann Richards — a young Australian actress who would make her name in Dieterle's *Love Letters* — and Walter Abel, one with which, today, he is happier than at the time. Perhaps because of his dissatisfaction with the cast, the actors in *An American Romance* seem even more subservient to the landscape than usual. It is a film of almost stylized simplicity, reducing Vidor's preoccupations to the simple conjunction of one man and the industrial landscape. Emerging blinking from the immigrant boat, Steve Dangloss makes his way alone, mostly on foot, to the steel country, where he confronts the might of American industry in the form of a simple symbol, another lone European (John Qualen) tearing at a hillside with a steam shovel. Thereafter, it immerses him — almost literally when molten metal slops down on him from a ladle as he stands trapped in a pit — and Vidor's documentation of the steel mills of Gary and Duluth gains an extra dimension from the presence of Dangloss, who personifies the conflict between man and nature.

Trimmed of thirty minutes by MGM, *An American Romance* lacks some spectacular action scenes (including one in which Dangloss slips down an ore chute into a ship's hold) as well as the incidental detail of his marriage to the schoolteacher Anna, the growth of his family, and his daughter's marriage which might have made it less of a stylized spectacular. In the shortened film, Dangloss rockets to magnatehood, designing a new automobile, branching out into aircraft and in time tooling America for war, all in the course of a few scenes, but the final effect is to dramatize with typical Vidor romanticism the possibilities for victory in the battle with nature if only, like Rogers in *Northwest Passage* and Roark in *The Fountainhead*, one will sacrifice all and not be swerved.

Vidor with aircraft workers during filming of
An American Romance

That Vidor may have seen himself in the same light as these mythical characters is suggested by his frequent confrontations with Hollywood's most domineering moguls, men with whom no director could hope to work except with a maximum of friction. Sam Goldwyn, Irving Thalberg and David Selznick totally opposed Vidor on three matters closest to his heart, Goldwyn in the creation of screenplays, Thalberg in his subservience to popular appeal, Selznick in the choice of locations. Yet it was for these three men that Vidor created his best work. "One often has to make films just to keep one's name in the public eye," he remarks, but the rationalization is thin. It is far more likely that only while working with such men was he pressured to do his best.

The hand of Selznick lies heavily but not without a sureness of touch on *Duel in the Sun* (1946), perhaps the greatest outdoor film of the forties. Niven Busch's novel had all Vidor's preoccupations, in particular a conflict between Man, in the person of Senator McCanles (Lionel Barrymore), a crippled monument in a wheelchair, and Nature, dramatized by his vast ranch, Spanish Bit. Industry — in this case the railroad — invades this empire, helped by

Duel in the Sun

McCanles's gentle son Jess (Joseph Cotten) but opposed, in imitation of his father, by the libidinous and violent Lewt (Gregory Peck). The innocently erotic Pearl Chavez (Jennifer Jones), an orphan half-caste billeted with the family after the execution of her father for her mother's murder, is flung from the protective Mrs. McCanles, played with a sense of gossamer and steel by Lillian Gish, to the affection of Jess and (her own preference) the satyriasis of Lewt, with whom she perishes in a demon tryst high in the mountains, both of them shot and dying together.

It is impossible not to be exhilarated by *Duel in the Sun*, in which Selznick tried with typical single-mindedness to recapture the scope and vivacity of *Gone With the Wind*. The interference of which Vidor complained added significantly to the film's success, but Vidor found the constant presence of Selznick on the set galling and walked out when the film was not quite completed.

Gregory Peck and Charles Bickford in ***Duel in the Sun***

Selznick directed some remaining scenes, William Dieterle handled a Reinhardtesque sequence in the vast bar which opens the film, and second-unit director Otto Brower the train wreck from which Lewt rides away singing, "I've Been Working On The Railroad." Even Josef von Sternberg, hired by Selznick to supervise the costume tests and, hopefully, give Jennifer Jones some of the photographic glamour of Marlene Dietrich — Vidor used him as an assistant, having him douse the star with water in scenes requiring the appearance of sweat — directed one brief scene of a posse searching the McCanles house. So acute was Selznick's obsession with his star that his visits to the set became embarrassing, the microphone picking up his heavy breathing as he watched her. Equally upsetting was a brief visit by D. W. Griffith. "Lionel Barrymore and Lillian Gish were incapable of speaking their script, especially Barrymore. After a moment I had to ask Mr. Griffith, 'Would you mind leaving the set or going behind the decor?' and he said, 'I'm sorry. I've been here too long anyway, I apologize.' And he left very politely."

After *Duel in the Sun*, Vidor had a long spell of inactivity, briefly broken by the sketch film *A Miracle Can Happen* (1948), also known as *On Our Merry Way*. Its personnel is a catalogue of renegades. Vidor codirected with Leslie Fenton, from a script by Laurence Stallings and Lou Breslow based on a story by Arch Oboler, best known for his radio work and science fiction films. One of Hollywood's slipperiest executives, Benedict Bogeaus, coproduced with star Burgess Meredith, who plays a reporter opposite Paulette Goddard in the thin linking story. Most of the stars — Dorothy Lamour, James Stewart, Henry Fonda, Harry James, Fred MacMurray — were war-time "names" whose popularity had slipped in the post-war slump and who were free to work for this low-budget United Artists release. Little of the film bears serious consideration, except a mild version of O. Henry's *The Ransom of Red Chief* with MacMurray and William Demarest, and a much-praised sketch (written by John O'Hara) for Fonda and Stewart as band musicians involved in a musical contest. Today Vidor chooses to ignore the film and pointedly omitted it from his filmographies. He is equally terse about his next project. Even though it was to become one of his most famous and distinguished films, he remarks only "In 1948 I accepted an assignment from Warner Brothers to direct a film, starring Gary Cooper, based on the controversial novel *The Fountainhead* by Ayn Rand."

When I remarked that the central impression of *The Fountainhead* is one of stylization, Vidor said, "I'm glad to hear you say that. It's just what I had in mind." He seldom worked with simpler materials nor made such remarkable use of them, achieving effects the accuracy of which he could sometimes only guess at. Imagining the hallucinating impression, for instance, of the Manhattan skyline seen through an ambulance window by a dying man, he shot Henry Hull's ride to the hospital from his point of view, the peaks of the skyscrapers reeling by beyond the painted cross. "And only a few years ago I was taken to the hospital. Looking out the win-

Patricia Neal and Gary Cooper in **The Fountainhead**

Vidor directs Neal and Cooper in ***The Fountainhead***

dow I saw the buildings exactly as I had made them appear in that scene."

In *The Crowd,* Vidor had affirmed his vision of the city as an extension of nature, relentless, severe, a jealous and fickle god, an image that reached its fruition in *The Fountainhead,* where New York's skyscrapers are the film's real focus, rather than the character of Howard Roark (Gary Cooper), the uncompromising architect who destroys his work rather than see its purity impaired. Before the film, Vidor studied the buildings of Frank Lloyd Wright, allegedly the model for Roark, but Cooper's performance, reflecting little of the crusty, philosophizing Wright, belongs with the heroes of other Vidor films; the half-controlled ferocity of Rogers, the indomitability of Dangloss, the dumb persistence of Jim Apperson in *The Big Parade* and of John Sims in *The Crowd,* the idealism of Doctor Manson in *The Citadel* all appear in Howard Roark, and Dominique Wynant (Patricia Neal) compresses all the unromantic but sexually aggressive heroines of earlier films. *The Fountainhead* has spectacular scenes of erotic tension, which fed on the unexpected attraction of the co-stars. "I drove her to Fresno," Vidor recollected of Patricia Neal, "and as soon as she and Cooper met, they went at one another. I guess it happened at dinner that night, because the next day it was all on." This mutual passion communicates itself superbly in the bedroom scene where Roark, reduced to working in a stone quarry, is summoned by Dominique to replace a flagstone she has intentionally broken. Attraction has been established in an earlier scene in which she visits the quarry, lusting covertly after the indifferent Roark as he drives the spike of a jackhammer into the leaning wall of stone, and in her boudoir, a space dissolved in mirrors and shadows, the calm shatters like a pane of glass. But for all its sexual tension, *The Fountainhead*'s most remarkable quality is the stylization at which Vidor so accurately aimed. Partly because of a low budget, most of the buildings are reduced to simple, elegant abstractions, rooms to harmonious geometrical arrangements of objects. Some rooms do not exist at all, but are merely suggested; one of his favorite effects, learned, Vidor acknowledged, from his studies of German painting, is to create with perspective and lighting an effect of space where none exists. Hospitals in *The Big Parade, Japanese War Bride* and *The Crowd* — clearly Vidor regards them as particularly impersonal — are created on empty stages with a few beds leading off in forced perspective, an effect used in *The Fountainhead* for a deserted newspaper office. Even more apt is the symbolism of objects or their absence; telegraphing her self-reliance, Dominique arrives at a party without that most essential of feminine props, a handbag, while the emptiness of her marriage to newspaper baron Gail Wynant (Raymond Massey) is conveyed by a lamp whose transparent base contains a trapped fish. Many of the script's lines read even more flatly than one thought possible even for Miss Rand — "I play the stockmarket of the spirit and I sell short," remarks architecture critic Ellsworth Toohey (Robert Douglas) with heavy significance — but in its stark invention and the flamboyant finale in which Roark stands atop a phallic skyscraper while Dominique races to meet him, one sees Vidor at his paradoxical best.

"SHE CANNOT FORGIVE, BUT SHE CAN GO ON FIGHTING":

RUBY GENTRY TO WAR AND PEACE

Although Vidor tried to sustain the fever of *The Fountainhead* in his next film, *Beyond the Forest* (1949), another subject in which soul and life were counters in an abstract game with the elemental forces of the earth, there was an inevitable sense of anti-climax. Bette Davis disliked her role of Rosa Moline, the dissatisfied wife of a small town doctor who itches to escape from the boredom of Loyalton, Wisconsin — "Like sitting in a coffin and waiting to be carried out" — to the glamour of Chicago and her industrialist lover. She battled with Vidor constantly, and used her irritation as a lever to evade the rest of her Warner Brothers contract; Warners happily freed the aging star, and she escaped from the burden of roles like that of Rosa which mocked her increasingly middle-aged appearance. With Joseph Cotten as the glum, unforceful doctor and Miss Davis inappropriately dressed in the *faux naive* rural wardrobe of off-the-shoulder blouses and peasant skirts worn by Jennifer Jones as Pearl Chavez, one can see *Beyond the Forest* as an exploration of the misery inevitably attendant on the marriage of Pearl and Jess in *Duel in the Sun* had Lewt not short-circuited the liaison, but the film's real preoccupation, as usual, is industry. If, in *The Fountainhead* and *An American Romance*, man domi-

Bette Davis in ***Beyond the Forest***

nates nature through industry, in *Beyond the Forest* the machine has total ascendancy: Loyalton's lumber works bathe the night sky in a perpetual glare, Rosa's beloved Chicago is a miserable and alien web of streets with her lover segregated in a Roark-type skyscraper she cannot penetrate, and her death from peritonitis following a crudely induced miscarriage — she jumps from a speeding car — is one of the greatest confrontations between woman and demon lover in all Vidor's films. As she drags herself from her sick bed towards escape and certain death, her tryst is not with a man but with a monstrous locomotive streaming steam from every orifice, snorting like a brute as the furnaces flood the sky with light.

Lightning Strikes Twice (1950), hardly recognizable as a Vidor film except in its desert setting and the bizarre central situation,

Richard Todd and Ruth Roman in **Lightning Strikes Twice**

has more affinities with traditional Warners melodrama — *Mildred Pierce, Humoresque* — and would have been better directed by Curtiz or Negulesco. British actor Richard Todd looks uncomfortable as the rancher acquitted of his wife's murder, Mercedes McCambridge performs with her usual mannerism as the woman responsible for his alibi, and Ruth Roman seldom knows what a mare's nest she has stumbled into. On the other hand, *Japanese War Bride* (1951), though a film Vidor dislikes, is a quiet and satisfying minor addition to his work, playing with a light touch on familiar preoccupations. American casualty Don Taylor marries his nurse Tae (Shirley Yamaguchi), takes her back to a Californian seaside home and, in time, makes her part of the community, conquering his own doubts as well as those of his family and the jealous xenophobia of his sister-in-law. Brought in when the film was almost fully prepared, Vidor had little time to work on the script, but the pale documentary quality of the images, the evocation of the market garden business with its strong contingent of Japanese owners, all bitterly resenting their wartime internment, the seaside location (used, inevitably, as a background for the most important scenes, including Tae's attempted suicide) and the evocations of tensions between man and his natural environment all contribute a sense of underlying tension, seldom tapped, unfortunately, by the routine acting. Vidor regards the scenes of lettuce packing as the film's main claim to remembrance.

Vidor returned to Selznick for his next film, the wild and remarkable *Ruby Gentry* (1952), Vidor's last great film. Due in the main to Jennifer Jones's performance as the self-destroying Southern girl who ruins the lives of those around her in a frantic attempt to achieve a satisfaction only death can bring, Vidor has called *Ruby Gentry* one of his favorite works. "I had complete freedom in shooting it, and Selznick, who could have had an influence on Jennifer Jones, didn't intervene. I think I succeeded in getting something out of Jennifer, something quite profound and subtle." Like *Beyond the Forest, Ruby Gentry* explores the eroticism and violence present in a small town (Braddock, South Carolina). To Vidor, the city is a battleground where an attempt to subdue nature has devitalized man and made his life futile. Only in the country, and particularly in his native South, is the battle still in full swing; there man still has a chance to prevail. Like Rosa Moline, Ruby comes "from the wrong side of the tracks." Despite her love for Boake Tackman (Charlton Heston), the last survivor of a decayed aristocratic line, she marries the gentle widower Jim Gentry (Karl Malden), whom she annihilates in her affair with Boake, the lover she in turn destroys by flooding the land he has reclaimed from the swamp. But to Vidor the swamp is eternal, unavoidable, and it

Charlton Heston and Jennifer Jones in ***Ruby Gentry***

is in the mud that Ruby and Boake hunt one another in perhaps the best sequence he ever filmed. Unable to afford a real location, Selznick recreated the swamp from *Hallelujah* on a sound stage, and the result, with its mist and shrouded, twisted trees is an apt model of the bog of human subconscious.

Jones and Heston give a remarkable ensemble performance, meeting one another's sexuality and violence with ever greater force, kiss for kiss, shot for shot. Ruby expertly handling a shotgun in her casually erotic male clothing, Tackman making an odd contrast with the mild, self-made Gentry; all could be characters from a Gothic novel, operating on emotions possible only in the life-

or-death environment of the South. Vidor later remarked that the film reminded him of Tennessee Williams, and allowing for the imposed simplicity of the material, the parallels are notable. He disliked the characters of the doctor (Bernard Phillips) and Ruby's fundamentalist bible-quoting brother Jewel (James Anderson), both forced on him by Selznick, but acknowledges their value in providing a perspective on Ruby's obsession to escape from Braddock. "The character of the brother interested me, as did that of Ruby's father, incidentally, because he was a prisoner of his environment. Unlike her father and brother, the girl proves she can get out of it. She bears deep scars, she's marked by this environment, also by the fact that she nourishes a fierce hatred in her breast. She cannot forgive, but she can go on fighting," — as can all Vidor's heroines, even though it means destroying the thing they love.

Paradoxically, Vidor has never found the Western, the most landscape-oriented of all American film forms, a congenial one, preferring landscape as a background to more personal sexual situations. Made in the wake of *Shane* (a film he greatly admires), *Man Without a Star* (1954) shares a familiar background; the battle between homesteaders and ranchers, with Kirk Douglas as the travelling gunman who, though hired initially by ranch owner Jeanne Crain, becomes in time an ally of the hated farmers, a decision for which he is brutally punished. Trapped by Crain's cowboys, he is trussed with barbed wire and dumped in the town's main street. Douglas's charmingly lecherous performance, the sexual motif and some of the location shooting is apt, but on the whole *Man Without a Star* is a minor work.

For a man who had in his time been offered both *Ben Hur* and *Gone With the Wind* Vidor made few real epics, but in the sixties he accepted two of the then-fashionable spectaculars, both creditable exercises in the contrast between man and nature. *War and Peace* (1955), produced by Dino De Laurentiis and shot on location in Italy, boiled down Tolstoy into four hours, though in most places the film was cut to less than three, mutilating what was already a condensed and simplified version of his canvas. Audrey Hepburn as Natasha considerably outdistanced Henry Fonda's languid, puzzled Pierre and Mel Ferrer's neutral Andrei;

Richard Boone and Kirk Douglas in **Man Without a Star**

War and Peace

he was then married to Miss Hepburn. "Someone once asked me if I would rather direct a battle scene with six thousand soldiers or a love scene with two important stars," Vidor said. "Without hesitating I answer, 'the battle scene.' " Vidor was referring to the problems of motivating actors, but he obviously reflects a general interest in spectacle and the exteriorizing of emotions which is typical of his work. The battles of *War and Peace* are spectacular enough, particularly the crossing of the river by the fleeing French, but the film's intimate moments suffer from Vidor's lack of interest in conventional characterization. Most interiors are well-lit arrangements of antiques, the actors included, and Vidor discards even the most alluring opportunities for personal drama. Natasha's appearance at the ball passes in a series of routine set-ups, even her soliloquies about the disappointment of having no partner being thrown away in a voice-over. British cinematographer Jack Cardiff

War and Peace

photographs the film with a golden tone reminiscent of his work on Michael Powell's *Black Narcissus,* and is largely responsible for the film's most memorable scene, the duel in the snow between Pierre and Kuragin, with the sun a red disc low on the horizon and the snow gleaming sickly with yellow light. The direction, mainly in long shot, takes advantage of the wide screen, and its impact is all the more remarkable for the fact that the whole scene is shot on a sound stage, the sun a reflection of a masked spotlight in a piece of glass placed only a few inches from the lens.

Audrey Hepburn in **War and Peace**

After *War and Peace,* producers offered Vidor a variety of epic subjects. Samuel Bronston urged him to direct *King of Kings* (directed by Nicholas Ray in 1961) and with Samuel Goldwyn Jr. he worked on the script of *Cervantes,* though when Goldwyn proved as intransigent as his father on the question of directors writing their own scripts, Vidor abandoned the project. In 1958, he took on the unpromising subject of *Solomon and Sheba* (1959) in which Tyrone Power starred opposite the temperamental Gina Lollobrigida. Disaster dogged the film. Producer Edward Small spent ten days in Spain casting the film, then left for good. With only half the footage shot, Power suffered the first of his eventually fatal heart attacks, and Yul Brynner took over in the lead. "The core of the story was Solomon's inner struggle to choose between his responsibilities as head of state and church and his yearning to satisfy his sensual desires with the Pagan queen," Vidor said. "Tyrone Power had understood the dualistic problem of the anguished king. When Brynner took over after his death, he fought the idea of a troubled monarch and wanted to dominate each situation without conflict. It was an attitude that affected the depth of his performance and probably the integrity of the film." Miss Lollobrigida also took her tone from Brynner and the production ended in confusion. Aside from some spectacular battles and a remarkable scene of horsemen plunging over a precipice, *Solomon*

Gina Lollobrigida in ***Solomon and Sheba***

and Sheba is a routine epic, though it possessed the potential to be as remarkable a blending of the personal and the panoramic as Mann's *El Cid*.

It is both ironic and appropriate that Vidor's last film should be a Biblical story; ironic in that his favorite motif, the swamp, had dried by the end of his career into a desert, and appropriate in that it legitimizes the many Biblical resonances in his earlier work. Devoted to Christian Science, he nevertheless founded his career on precepts which echo the Bible's darker admonitions, characterized by his 1920 "Creed and Pledge" and by the frequent "preachments" of his work. To have chosen a creed which put the Bible's philosophy into a usable and functional form was characteristic of a man who has always believed that action is better than words, progress better than stasis. The burden of all his advice to young artists is a simple, "You've got to keep working."

His vision and philosophy are compressed in one Biblical story, that of Job. Even the visual references have a relationship to Vidor's work. Satan appears before God and, in answer to his "Whence comest thou?," replies, "From going to and fro in the earth, and from walking up and down in it," a precise evocation of Vidor's sense that the soil is a domain of evil. Job is destroyed by an impersonal destiny as part of a cosmic experiment but, finally indomitable, is rewarded for his fortitude. With its evocation of a world where water, lightning and animals trumpet the dominance and glory of God, the book of Job reflects the combination of stubbornness, mysticism and sensual appreciation of nature that makes the work of King Vidor one of the great ornaments of the American cinema.

FILMOGRAPHY

1919 THE TURN IN THE ROAD
BETTER TIMES
THE OTHER HALF
POOR RELATIONS

1920 THE JACK KNIFE MAN
THE FAMILY HONOR

1921 THE SKY PILOT
LOVE NEVER DIES

1922 CONQUERING THE WOMAN
WOMAN, WAKE UP
THE REAL ADVENTURE
DUSK TO DAWN
ALICE ADAMS (produced)

1923 PEG O' MY HEART
THE WOMAN OF BRONZE
THREE WISE FOOLS

1924	WILD ORANGES HAPPINESS WINE OF YOUTH HIS HOUR
1925	WIFE OF THE CENTAUR PROUD FLESH THE BIG PARADE
1926	LA BOHEME BARDELYS THE MAGNIFICENT
1928	THE CROWD THE PATSY SHOW PEOPLE
1929	HALLELUJAH
1930	NOT SO DUMB BILLY THE KID
1931	STREET SCENE THE CHAMP
1932	BIRD OF PARADISE CYNARA
1933	THE STRANGER'S RETURN
1934	OUR DAILY BREAD
1935	THE WEDDING NIGHT SO RED THE ROSE
1936	THE TEXAS RANGERS
1937	STELLA DALLAS

1938 THE CITADEL

1940 NORTHWEST PASSAGE
COMRADE X

1941 H.M. PULHAM ESQ.

1944 AN AMERICAN ROMANCE

1946 DUEL IN THE SUN

1948 A MIRACLE CAN HAPPEN (ON OUR MERRY WAY, co-director Leslie Fenton)

1949 THE FOUNTAINHEAD
BEYOND THE FOREST

1951 LIGHTNING STRIKES TWICE

1952 JAPANESE WAR BRIDE
RUBY GENTRY

1955 MAN WITHOUT A STAR

1956 WAR AND PEACE

1959 SOLOMON AND SHEBA

OTHER PROJECTS

In addition to his early short films, Vidor completed during the sixties the 26-minute *Truth and Illusion: An Introduction to Metaphysics*, a documentary which he shot and narrated. He has also made a short documentary about his home town Paso Robles.

The Yearling and the second half of *Northwest Passage* were not Vidor's only uncompleted films. Film exhibitor Sid Graumann, a fellow Christian Scientist, bought the rights to *The Turn in the Road* which Vidor hoped to remake as *The Milly Story,* but this was never made. He hoped to remake *The Crowd* and also to film the life story of James Murray, its ill-fated star. In the fifties, Vidor wanted to launch a film of Hawthorne's *The Marble Faun,* and Merian Cooper approached him to direct *The Land,* a Cinerama spectacular; Vidor withdrew when he found MGM's ex-boss Louis B. Mayer had an interest in the Cinerama Corporation. In addition to *Cervantes,* which was to have been made by Samuel Goldwyn Jr., Samuel Bronston offered Vidor *King of Kings* and Howard Hughes the biblical subject *Pilate's Wife,* from an idea by Clare Boothe Luce.

Of Vidor's brief television career, Herbert Luft writes: "In the spring of 1953 Vidor joined three other top feature-film directors in a venture to make a series of hour-long films for television release. However, since they had to guarantee 39 films a year for a complete series, they abandoned the project — 39 good stories could not be found that fast. The idea of 'pay television' came up and there was great confusion. King Vidor finally did television around 1954, directing the major portion of *Light's Golden Jubilee*, a two-hour spectacular sponsored by General Electric and produced by David O. Selznick. Vidor was especially pleased with the assignment because it proved that there was no hard feeling between Selznick and himself."

SELECTIVE BIBLIOGRAPHY

Barr, C. "King Vidor." *Brighton* 21:22, March 1970.
Beach, B. "Interview." *Motion Picture Classic* 10:22, June 1928.
"Biographical note; filmog." *Movies and People* 2:46, 1940.
Braver-Mann, B. G. "Vidor and Evasion." *Experimental Cinema* 1-3, Fall 1931.
Brownlow, K. "King Vidor." *Film* 34:19 (Lon), Winter 1962.
Cheatham, M. "Interview." *Motion Picture Classic* 10:22, June 1928.
Daugherty, F. "Steel Comes to the Films; Vidor's Film America." *Christian Science Mon. Magazine*, p. 8, May 8, 1943.
"Early Steps to Success." *Motion Picture Classic* 8:24, August 1919.
Greenberg, J. "War, Wheat and Steel; Interview." *Sight and Sound* 37-4:192, Autumn 1968.
Griffith, R. "Sovereign Audience." *Saturday Review* 36:23, October 24, 1953.
Harrington, C. "King Vidor's Hollywood Progress." *Sight and Sound* 22-4:179, April/June 1953.
Higham, C. "Long Live Vidor, a Hollywood King." *New York Times*, Sec. 2:1, September 3, 1972.
Higham, C. "King Vidor." *Film Heritage* 1-4, Summer 1966.
"King Vidor's America." *Lions Roar* 3-4, July 1944.
"King Vidor at New York University; Discussion." *Cineaste* 1-4, Spring 1968.

Luft, H. G. "A Career that Spans Half a Century." *The Film Journal* 1-2:27, Summer 1971.
Lyons, D. aud O'Brien, G. "King Vidor; filmog." *Interview* 26:12, October 1972.
"Man Who Did It." *Newsweek* 48:53, July 30, 1956.
Mitchell, G. J. "King Vidor." *Films in Review* 15-3:179, March 1964.
Orme, M. "Genius of Realism." *Illustrated London N* 180:12, January 2, 1932.
Perkins, V. F. and Shivas, M. "Interview." *Movie* 11:7, July/August, 1963.
Smith, F. J. "Tells How *The Big Parade* was Made." *Motion Picture Classic* 23:26, May 1926.
"Special Vidor Issue." *Positif*, September 1974.
St. Johns, A. R. "A Young Crusader." *Photoplay* 17-1:64, December 1919.
———. "Story of." *Photoplay* 24:28, August 1923.
"The Big Screens." *Sight and Sound* 24-4: 209, Spring 1955.
Trumbo, D. "Stepchild of the Muse." *North American* R D 1933.
Tully, J. "Interview." *Vanity Fair* 26:46, June 1926.
Vidor, K. and Brooks, R. "Two Story Conferences." *Sight and Sound 22-2:85*, October/December 1952.
Vidor, K. *A Tree Is a Tree*. New York: Harcourt Brace, 1952.
———. "Bringing Pulham to the Screen." *Lions Roar* 1-4, December 1941.
———. "Director's Notebook — Why Teach Cinema?" *Cinema Progress* 4-1/2:2, June/July 1939.
———. "Me . . . and My Spectacle." *Films and Filming* 6-1:6, October 1959.
———. *On Film Making*. London: W. H. Allen, 1973.
———. "Rubber Stamp Movies." *New Theatre*, September 1934.
———. "The Story Conference."*Films In Review* 3-6:266, June/July 1952.
Weller, S. M. "Interview." *Motion Picture Classic* 26:23, Spring 1927.